ELSTON

ELSTON

THE STORY OF THE
FIRST AFRICAN-AMERICAN YANKEE

ARLENE HOWARD
AND
RALPH WIMBISH

Guilford, Connecticut

An imprint of Globe Pequot

Distributed by NATIONAL BOOK NETWORK

Copyright © 2018 The Curators of the University of Missouri
Originally published in 2001 as *Elston and Me* by the University of Missouri Press

British Library Cataloguing in Publication Information available

A previous paperback edition was catalogued by the Library of Congress as follows:

Library of Congress Cataloging-in-Publication Data
Howard, Arlene.
   Elston and me : the story of the first Black Yankee / Arlene
Howard and Ralph Wimbish.
   p. cm.
   Includes bibliographical references and index.
1. Howard, Elston, b. 1930. 2. Baseball players—United States—Biography. 3. African American baseball players—Biography. 4. Howard, Arlene. 5. Baseball players' spouses—United States—Biography. 6. New York Yankees (Baseball team)—History. I. Wimbish, Ralph. II. Title.
GV865.H65 H69 2001
796.357'092—dc21
[B]   2001041584

ISBN 0-8262-1358-8 (alk. paper)
ISBN 978-1-4930-2900-6 (paperback)
ISBN 978-1-4930-2901-3 (e-book)

∞™ The paper used in this publication meets the minimum requirements of American National Standard for Information Sciences—Permanence of Paper for Printed Library Materials, ANSI/ NISO Z39.48-1992.

Printed in the United States of America

Contents

CONTENTS

FOREWORD

by Don Newcombe

TO SAY WHAT TYPE OF HUMAN BEING ELSTON HOWARD WAS, I WOULD
have to start with Jackie Robinson. Jackie was a person I always described
with three letters—M-A-N. Elston Howard was the same kind of person
Jackie Robinson was. He was a MAN.

Elston and I were good friends. We were opponents only on the
baseball field. We only got to see each other in spring training or when
the Dodgers and Yankees played each other in the World Series. We had
a couple of confrontations while he was with the Yankees, and he hit
some bombs off me.

I often think back on how it was for Elston when he first joined the
Yankees. They didn't want a black man on the Yankees even though the
Dodgers had Jackie and had broken down the color barrier. The Yankees
didn't want Elston, because of the innate prejudice at the time on that
ball club and in that organization. And when Elston came, what he had
to go through is somewhat the same as what Jackie had to face. I felt for
Elston, because he was by himself to a degree. Larry Doby, of course, had
broken the color barrier in the American League in 1948, and it should
have been easier for Elston when he came along in 1955, but it wasn't.

He was an outstanding baseball player, an outstanding person, a man
who made history. Elston should have been given more publicity in New
York, the biggest media market in the world. They seemed to want to
hold him down when he first got there. And Elston had to prove himself
over and over again.

Elston hit two home runs off me in the World Series. In 1955, he
homered off me in his first World Series at-bat. The pitch I threw in 1956

was a fastball, and just a case of getting it in the wrong spot. In that 1956 series, you know, I had good luck with Mickey Mantle. I struck him out twice, but Yogi Berra hit two home runs and Elston, of course, hit one. He was one of the greatest competitors I ever faced on the field, and we became good friends.

Elston Howard was a class act off the field as well. He moved into an area in Teaneck, New Jersey, he and his wife, Arlene, and their family. And he was respected and was one of the first black people to move into that community. Believe me, thinking back on my career and my life, I often thank God I was given the chance to play with people like Jackie Robinson and Roy Campanella and given the good fortune to play against people like Elston Howard. They were class people.

But there's more to it than being a renowned person with a uniform on or standing on the stage and doing whatever you do with your talent. It's what you do when you leave that stage or leave that arena that tells in my opinion their true character. Do you sign autographs for kids? Do you stay away from drugs? Do you stay away from abusing alcohol? Do you care about people? That's the type of person I am talking about, and the category that I put Elston Howard in. I thank God I was able to pass Elston Howard's way and have a chance to know him as a person—much the same as I did with Jackie Robinson.

—Don Newcombe, courtesy of Tom Reed,
Members Only Television

FOREWORD

by Yogi Berra

ONE OF THE GREAT THINGS ABOUT THE YANKEES WAS BEING PART OF something special and playing with great players. We always pulled for each other; there were no jealousies, only great teammates. That's why I'll always treasure the friends I made in my seventeen years with the Yankees—especially Ellie Howard.

Ellie was truly one of the greatest guys I ever knew. We became very good friends, as did our wives. For years, Ellie and I would often eat and even shop together—so did Carm and Arlene, who were very good pals. I remember they used to laugh at the clothes Ellie and I would buy on the road.

Ellie was a high-class guy, and a darn good ballplayer. We had several things in common—we both came from St. Louis, were catchers, and made room for each other moving to the outfield. I don't remember Ellie ever griping or complaining about anything. I knew he faced some prejudice in spring training and probably felt a burden as the first black Yankee. But Ellie never caused any controversy—he was always pleasant to be around.

When Ellie first came up in 1955, no one on the Yankees really cared that he was the first black on our team. It wasn't a big deal. What mattered was that he was a good man who could help our team. When a bunch of us went out to eat, we'd always make sure Ellie came along. I think he felt comfortable as a Yankee. Moose Skowron, myself, Phil Rizzuto, Mickey Mantle, all of us loved Ellie as our teammate.

I was still going good in '55—I won the MVP that year—but Ellie as a rookie was too good to keep out of the lineup. So Casey Stengel put him in left field. And it stayed that way for a few years. Bill Dickey used to work with Ellie, like he had done with me years earlier, and I think that helped. By 1960 they started putting me in the outfield more and Ellie behind the plate. He was the complete catcher—he did everything great. I remember Ryne Duren, who had bad eyesight, couldn't see Ellie's hand signals so Ellie would signal the pitch by the number of crouches he'd make.

Ellie had a lot of smarts and would've been a great manager. He really knew the game; he knew how to handle people. When we coached together with the Yankees, I know everyone respected his knowledge.

If you were Elston Howard's teammate, you were a friend for life. In my museum at Montclair State University, one of my favorite pictures on the wall shows me with Ellie as he happily shared in the occasion of my two thousandth career hit. That was really special. So is one of those inscribed bricks that Arlene was the first to buy when we built the museum. The brick lies directly in front of the museum and says, "Elston Gene Howard." If there were room, I'd add, "A great Yankee. A great friend."

—Yogi Berra

PREFACE

Ralph Wimbish

A man of great gentleness and dignity . . . One of the all-time Yankee greats . . . American League MVP in 1963 . . . Winner of two Gold Gloves . . . A fitting leader to be the first black player to wear the Yankee uniform . . . If indeed humility is a trademark of many great men—Elston Howard was one of the truly great Yankees.

AMONG THE MONUMENTS AT YANKEE STADIUM HONORING THE BASE-ball greats who have had their uniform numbers retired by the New York Yankees, there is a plaque. This is where you will find the testament to the spirit of the late Elston Howard, the first black Yankee.

Arlene Henley Howard was his wife, and this book is their story. Maybe Arlene, too, deserves a plaque, for together, she and Elston made history. Theirs was a partnership in which Elston committed his life to baseball while Arlene raised their three children and remained the driving force in his career. A lady of elegance, she herself showed amazing dignity back in the turbulent 1950s and 1960s, when black wives were new to baseball. Even then, Arlene was never afraid to speak up about the injustices she saw around her.

The Howard home was Arlene's ballpark, and she was the star. With Elston often away on road trips with the team, she kept their household together, raised three beautiful children, and even handled Elston's contracts. Her challenges were compounded over the years by the burden of diabetes as well as the need to care for their youngest daughter, Karen, who was born with cerebral palsy.

As the years went by, the challenges became greater. Health problems eventually resulted in the untimely deaths of Elston and two of their children. It is to Arlene's credit that she coped admirably with each tragedy. When Elston passed away in 1980 at the age of fifty-one from a rare heart disease, a condition she feels was brought on and hastened by the years of suppressing his emotions, she was suddenly cast in the role of family breadwinner. Immediately she involved herself in the family's fledgling printing business and transformed it into a successful company that earned millions of dollars.

Arlene has never forgotten the days in St. Louis, her hometown, where she and Elston grew up and fell in love. She remembers when the Yankees thumbed their noses at integration with an all-white lineup, years after Jackie Robinson had broken the color barrier. The Yankees responded to public criticism by claiming they were waiting for the right man, a black man of great moral character. Arlene's husband, Elston Howard, was that man.

In 1955 Elston became the first black to play for the New York Yankees. He was one of their most popular players—a winner who played in ten World Series and on nine All-Star teams. He played for the greatest team of all time, the 1961 Yankees. When his playing career ended, he so much wanted to be baseball's first black manager, but he was denied that opportunity.

It's a shame Elston does not have a plaque in baseball's Hall of Fame in Cooperstown, New York. Having a plaque of his own at Yankee Stadium and his number, 32, retired is not enough. There are only thirteen catchers in the Hall of Fame. Arguably, catching is the most important defensive position on the baseball field. Elston always said the catcher controls the game; he's the only player who has the entire field in front of him, and he calls every pitch. Yet at Cooperstown catchers remain the second-least-represented position, ahead of only third basemen.

Defensively, when you list the great catchers of the game—Johnny Bench, Roy Campanella, Bill Dickey, and Yogi Berra—Elston Howard ranks among the best of all time. He caught in more than one thousand games, and his .993 career fielding average remains among the highest at his position.

Similarly, his lifetime hitting statistics compare favorably to several players in the Hall of Fame. His career batting average (.279) is better than Phil Rizzuto's, Pee Wee Reese's, and Roy Campanella's.

Of all the great men to wear the Yankee pinstripes, he was the proudest of them all. Unlike some of his teammates, Elston truly lived up to the Yankee mystique. With remarkable temperament, restraint, and courage, he was the Jackie Robinson of baseball's most storied franchise. No Yankee ever carried himself with more dignity. No Yankee had greater respect for his teammates or love for his wife and family. And no one loved being a Yankee more than Elston Howard.

Now, more than twenty years after his death, Arlene feels it is time to tell their story. I was fortunate to know Elston when I was a little boy growing up in St. Petersburg, Florida. He was the greatest of my childhood heroes, one who actually slept at our home because he was barred from staying in the same spring-training hotel as his teammates. My father was the local NAACP leader who spoke out against the Jim Crow laws. Whenever he could not find Elston a decent place to sleep, he invited him to stay at our home, and I feel privileged that Elston Howard slept in my bedroom.

Throughout Elston's life, he never let his anger and frustrations get in the way of being a New York Yankee. Arlene likes to say he never got his due. She's right. He was a great man. A family man. A courageous man whose heart belonged to baseball. A man who belongs in the Hall of Fame.

The Funeral

Arlene Howard

THE CALL CAME RIGHT ABOUT MIDNIGHT. THE MAN ON THE PHONE—HE must have been a doctor—asked me if I could come back to the hospital. I said, "OK, I'll get ready," but then the voice said, "Hold on just a minute, maybe you don't have to come." I felt helpless, waiting there on the phone for a good minute or so. The voice finally returned and told me there was no need to come. My husband had passed away.

His death really was no surprise. The date was December 14, 1980, more than a year after Elston had been diagnosed with myocarditis, a rare disorder in which a virus attacks the muscles around the heart. Elston had been in Columbia Presbyterian, a New York hospital, for about a week. We were considering a heart transplant, but time had run out.

There was no time to cry. The next day I knew I had to make funeral arrangements. Elston had said if anything ever happened to him, do it quickly. He once told me the most ridiculous thing at a funeral is where they wait for a week before they bury you. He thought it was ridiculous to wait around. Elston said if it ever happened to him, he wanted to be buried the next day like they do in the Jewish religion. But I couldn't arrange it that fast. I wanted to allow my family and Elston's family to get here. He deserved that much. He deserved a funeral like Jackie Robinson's in 1972.

I called a good friend of mine, Daisy Batson, to help me with the arrangements. Years before we had owned an art gallery together and had lived on the same street when we first moved to Teaneck in 1958. I had a very good friend, Dr. Robert Ross Johnson, whom Elston and I knew socially. Since we didn't belong to a church at the time (I was Methodist, Elston was Baptist), he was our choice to handle the funeral service. I called our good friend Marian Logan. She was a friend of Duke Ellington's; she told me he wrote "Satin Doll" for her. Marian was known as "Jackie Robinson's sister" and played a major role in the arrangement of Jackie's funeral. That's the reason I called her. She agreed: Elston should have the best at his funeral. Why not? He was the first black man to play for the New York Yankees.

That Monday afternoon, Daisy went with me to Campbell's Funeral Home, and we made the arrangements. I called Marian back and told her I wanted to do this thing as soon as possible. Marian suggested I call the minister at Riverside Presbyterian, the same church where Jackie's funeral was held. Marian got a hold of Rev. George Thomas and made all the arrangements, lining up the choir, the pallbearers, things like that. The funeral service was set for Wednesday. I talked to Cedric Tallis about arranging the pallbearers. Mr. Tallis was the Yankees' general manager and had known Elston since the early '50s when Elston played in the minors at Kansas City. George Steinbrenner called and asked if there was anything he could do.

The previous year I had gone to Thurman Munson's funeral after he died in a plane crash, and I remembered how eloquently Bobby Murcer had read from Ecclesiastes at the service. I called Bill White—he and Elston were very good friends—and asked him to read the Scripture. I called Rev. Johnson, and he coordinated everything between the church and all those who would speak at the service.

On Tuesday my youngest daughter, Karen, was brought home. Then twenty-one years old, Karen had cerebral palsy. We'd sent her away to the Woods School in Pennsylvania, the finest boarding school in the area for young people with disabilities. The day after Elston died I called the school, but it was Karen's teacher who had to be the one to tell her that her father had died. I know she took it very badly; she loved him very much.

Our other two children, Cheryl and Elston Jr., had rushed home to Teaneck. Cheryl, then twenty-two, was on the road in Detroit performing with the road company of the Broadway play *They're Playing Our Song*. Elston Jr., then twenty-five, had a job selling insurance in Miami. It was very tough for him, because he had left home and gone to Florida a few weeks before without telling me or his father. By leaving home, he had broken his father's heart, and Elston Jr. never got to apologize to him.

My sisters, my nephews, my mother, they all came. I remember my mother saying, "Yeah, I gotta be there." My sister Loyette was on her way to Hawaii, so she couldn't make it. She told me she wanted to remember Elston the way he was: always smiling, so full of life.

On Tuesday afternoon, I got a call from the Yankee front office. Several of the players wanted to come early before the wake later that night. I said OK. By Wednesday morning, the day of the funeral, nearly all of my family was here and Elston's father, Travis, of course. It's interesting, I never thought about calling or including him in the service because he really had no part in Elston's life. He was a prominent educator in Missouri, but had never married Elston's mother. Travis never acknowledged Elston's existence until he became a major-league baseball star. He was nowhere in sight when Elston was born, but now here he was at our doorstep. Travis arrived the day before the funeral. In the house, we had no room for him, so Elston Jr. took him to a hotel nearby in Hackensack. That's where he stayed.

My oldest sister, Martha, and her family drove from St. Louis with my mother and didn't arrive until just minutes before the funeral. The limousines and hearses were outside when they drove up. There was no time to say hello. All they could do was get into the cars. Martha wanted to view the body, but the funeral home director said it was not possible. It was a cold, rainy day, but on the way to the service the sun broke through. I remember the big church, the service, walking down the aisle with Karen in the wheelchair, and looking at all the people there, including baseball commissioner Bowie Kuhn and Mike Burke, the former Yankee president. I remember seeing Dave Winfield come in; the Yankees had just signed him to a big contract. My godson from Florida, Orion

"Skipper" Ayer Jr., got to the church just as we were getting to the cars. I remember all the cars. Police cars from Hackensack and Bergen County were everywhere. We had a police escort.

At the church, the closed casket was flanked at the altar by a huge blue floral wreath in the shape of the Yankees' NY logo and a portrait by Pablo Carreno, a good friend of Elston's who had also done a painting of Roberto Clemente. We had sold a lot of his paintings at our gallery. Opera singer Robert Merrill sang "America the Beautiful." The pallbearers were Whitey Ford, Yogi Berra, Mickey Mantle, Monte Irvin, Ernie Banks, and Bill Dickey, every one of them a Hall of Famer. Many of Elston's Yankee teammates and friends were there: Phil Rizzuto, Dick Howser, Billy Martin, Bernie Miller and his wife, Fran. New York Governor Hugh Carey was there. So was Congressman Charles Rangel.

Whitey Ford, one of Elston's favorite teammates whom Elston had once dubbed "Chairman of the Board," was the first to speak. "When I found out late Saturday night of Elston passing away, I just stayed up all night," he said. "I didn't go back to sleep. I walked around the house, looked at pictures of Elston and me and our other teammates. I went through scrapbooks, and I just went back in time from 1955, when I first met him, and I thought of some of the bad times we've had and some of the good times.

"Some of the bad times, I guess, his first year with the Yankees, 1955. We won the pennant, two years before that we'd won five World Series in a row. I know Elston was dying to get that World Series ring, and we lost to the Dodgers that year. But the following year we came right back and won. Another thing I think Elston felt very sad about was a year or two after he joined the club two of his real close friends left the Yankees, Phil Rizzuto and Billy Martin. I think that was a low time in his life. Another time I remember, 1960, and the World Series in Pittsburgh, which we lost in seven games. I remember Elston getting hit by a pitch in the sixth game, early in the game, not being able to finish that game out, and then missing the seventh game, which we lost. Probably the only time I've ever seen Elston mad at an opposing player.

"The good times I try to remember: Elston was the Most Valuable Player in 1963. And then I think of him winning his first World Series in 1956. I think of him winning the Babe Ruth Award for the Most Valuable Player in the [1958] World Series. Those were the good times."

Whitey looked at the children and me and spoke about the time in 1962 when he and his wife and kids filmed a TV commercial for oatmeal with our family. He remembered how difficult it was because our kids wouldn't eat it. The kids refused to eat the oatmeal until we had thrown a bunch of bananas and sugar on it.

"Yes, he was quite a ballplayer," Whitey said. "But I think all his teammates over the years admire him more for the way he carried himself in hotels and on planes and on the trains. He just was such a gentleman, always carried himself well. I think his teammates—you have to remember he had hundreds of teammates on the Yankees in his long career—they admired him for the great courage he had, especially early in his career. I don't think even the fellows on our team back in 1955 and 1956 realized how tough Elston really had it. But he got through and he just did a great job. I think the big thing was his pride in being a Yankee, and no one exemplified it more than he did.

"So much dignity, so much class. Elston, we love you. We will pray for you and your family always. Number 32, rest in peace."

Reggie Jackson was the next speaker. He said there was "a certain kind of respect that radiated from Elston Howard. I am sure he was perused and scrutinized, selected by God, and selected by people on this earth to be the first [black] Yankee.

"Yes, he was a man of class. And one that taught and continued to teach and touch the younger generation that's his people, such as myself, what it meant to speak at the right time, to say the right things when it meant the most. How to be a positive influence, no matter who you associated yourself with, no matter what color you were. He was truly a person who I felt transcended any kind of particular denomination, and that's really the highest tribute I feel I can pay someone."

Bill White spoke of Elston's "great dignity and inner strength. A lot of people figured that Ellie fought for Ellie, but quietly he was responsible for many changes. He was a fighter in his own quiet way." White then read from Ecclesiastes 3:1–8. "For everything there is a season and a time for every matter under heaven, a time to be born, and a time to die . . ."

Robert Merrill sang "The Lord's Prayer." Rev. Johnson touched many hearts when he said in his benediction, "America is a better place because Elston Howard walked this land. Thank God for the joy of memory."

I don't remember whose idea it was, but I will never forget the funeral procession. You couldn't see the end of it, dozens of cars, all with their headlights on from the church, winding around Yankee Stadium, stretching the length of the George Washington Bridge and on to the cemetery in New Jersey. At the funeral site in Paramus, we didn't stay long. There was a large bunch of red roses, and I took them and gave them out individually to close friends and family.

For weeks and weeks, I was really numb. I lost seven or eight pounds because I couldn't eat anything and I couldn't sleep. It's the strangest thing when you can't sleep. I was so angry that he had died so young. We had so many good times. We had gone through so much together. There were tears, but I wouldn't cry in a crowd of people. When people would see me they would say, "What a strong person," but I did what I had to do. What alternative is there?

Lionel Reison, a partner in the Elston Howard Printing Company, thought it would be a good idea to get me involved in the business. Then one weekend we went to Atlantic City, just to get away from home, and that's when the house was robbed. It was about three months after the funeral. The robbers took all of Elston's jewelry, including his World Series rings, eight or nine of them. They took the one he had on his hand the night he died. It was the first one he got in 1955, and he always cherished that one the most. That was the one he always wore. None of the stuff taken was mine, just his. It was just there in our bedroom. I had left everything the way it was. Even after Elston died I never picked up any of those things. I never got rid of anything in his closet. It was at least two years before I did.

The doctors said a rare heart virus was responsible for Elston's death, but I believed he died from a broken heart. All those years he was never appreciated. Deep inside he never thought he was given credit for all he had accomplished. It was Elston's dream to be a major-league manager, baseball's first black manager. It was his vision, and he felt he was eminently qualified. But that dream of his never came true.

Jackie Robinson told me years ago how much he respected Elston because Elston had a tougher road to the majors than he. Jackie played for the Dodgers, a team that had sought him out, and Branch Rickey, the general manager, fully supported him. Elston had no such support from the Yankees. He grew up believing he had to be better than anyone else, and so he was. And he did it for the New York Yankees, the winningest team in baseball, a team that did not really want him. Five years after the Yankees had signed him, when Elston was twenty-six years old, they buckled under to local pressure in 1955 and reluctantly made him their Jackie Robinson.

The Yankees signed him in 1950, but always came up with an excuse to keep him in the minors. Unlike most major-league teams, the Yankees were in no hurry to integrate. They were winning without black players, so what did they need Elston for?

Buck O'Neil, Elston's manager in the Negro Leagues, wrote a book entitled *Right on Time*. In Elston's case, the timing was wrong. Five years earlier, he would have been one of the greatest players in Negro League history. Five years later, I believe undeniably he would have been one of major-league baseball's greatest players and one of its finest managers.

Elston's road to the major leagues is paved with wonderful memories, but there were plenty of bumps along the way. The journey started in a single-family household with a hardworking mother. It all began in St. Louis.

CHAPTER ONE

Compton Hill

Arlene and Elston always seemed to complement each other. She was the fire; he was the ice.

—BILL WHITE

I WAS THREE YEARS OLD WHEN MY FATHER, NATHAN HENLEY, PICKED me up and kissed me good-bye. It was 1936 and our family was living in Brownsville, Tennessee, a small town about eighty miles northeast of Memphis. My father was a tall, stubborn man who loved his family more than anything in this world. The country was in a depression. He knew there had to be a better life somewhere, anywhere but Brownsville. He was a sharecropper on a huge farm owned by my mother's father, Oliver Johnson. He was a Methodist minister. He told us stories about the time he saw Abraham Lincoln in a parade when he was a kid.

My mother was named Mattie. She, too, knew there had to be a better life someplace else, so she allowed Nathan to go off on his own. One morning he set off on foot for St. Louis, vowing to find a better job, a better place to live, with better schools for his children. He had no suitcase; only a pair of boots, overalls, and the shirt on his back.

In those days, St. Louis was nothing but one big factory. Smokestacks produced a thick haze that hung out over the Mississippi River; paradoxically, the same factories were a beacon of light to thousands of black people from all across the South. They saw the smoke as some sort of signal, an invitation not to be turned down. So they came any way they could, by train, by bus, by car, even by foot, from the cotton fields of Mississippi, Arkansas, and Tennessee, all with hopes of finding a better life.

A steady wave of black emigrants found their way to Compton Hill, a soot-splattered neighborhood on St. Louis's south side, its narrow streets packed with scores of industrial sites, corner churches, and rows and rows of red-brick tenement houses. The air was filled with the pungent smell of the Portland Cement and Scullin Steel plants. The neighborhood bustled with sweatshops and cluttered marketplaces; a constant grinding noise came from the railroad yard across LaSalle Street. To those with dreams, Compton Hill was home.

I was the fourth of Nathan Henley's five children. First there were my older sisters Martha and Loyette. Then came Nathaniel, myself, and baby brother Edwin. It was not easy for our mother to raise us while our father was away, but she managed with the help of my grandparents and Uncle Gilbert and Aunt Mary. With my father gone, my mother grew anxious, but all she could do was wait. About a week after he left, we got a letter postmarked from St. Louis. My father wrote to say he had found a job at a steel mill on the south side of town. On his first day there he had been standing outside the Sheffield Steel plant with a bunch of other men looking for work. A man came outside and began looking them over. He pointed to my father and said, "You there, in the back, come on up here." Just like that, my father had a job.

It took about two months, but my father eventually saved enough money to send for us. We came by train with everything we had. We stayed with Auntie Louise, my father's sister, in a three-room apartment on Chocteau Street for a few months until we got a place of our own at 1206 Theresa Street in the Compton Hill section of town.

My father had to work two jobs. He'd get up every morning at five and go to work at Sheffield Steel. At four in the afternoon he would go straight to his second job at the Century Foundry; he didn't come home until eleven. Every night around seven o'clock my brothers and sisters and I took turns taking him his dinner. Pot roast was his favorite. He would always have a big smile on his face when he'd see us arrive with a big basket of food. My mother worked, too. She had a part-time job as one of the salad girls at Lemon's, a fancy restaurant on the south side of town.

When he wasn't working, my father enjoyed being home. He was very concerned that we do our schoolwork and stay out of trouble. He also loved baseball. He occasionally would catch a St. Louis Stars game down at the Dust Bowl at Market and Grand, but he loved listening to the Cardinals on the radio. The Cardinals always had a good team; it seemed like they were in the World Series every year. I would listen to the games, too, just to please him, and that's how I became a baseball fan. I listened to Harry Caray, knew all the stats and batting averages. My father thought I was so smart.

He was especially happy when he heard the news about Jackie Robinson. To say Jackie Robinson brought a lot of pride to the black community is an understatement. Breaking the color barrier was a big thing in St. Louis. He was a role model like no other in black America. Teachers at our school constantly talked about him in our classrooms. If you showed up late for class, the teacher would say, "Jackie Robinson wouldn't be late." If you misbehaved, the teachers would say, "Jackie Robinson wouldn't act like that." And we believed every word.

In 1947 when Jackie Robinson and the Brooklyn Dodgers came to St. Louis for the first time to play against the Cardinals, it seemed like Sportsman's Park was jam-packed with just as many black faces as white ones. Black schools were closed. Local shops on LaSalle Street shut down early. It was like a big holiday.

Growing up, I didn't go to many baseball games, but I went to that game with my girlfriend Betty. We sat in what was known as the "knot-hole" section. We had heard so much about Jackie Robinson that I just had to go. We cheered when he ran out onto the field and every time he came to bat. When the game was over, we all waited for him outside the visiting locker room, as if he were a movie star. When he came outside, everyone began to cheer and ask for his autograph. As he made his way toward the team bus, I was able to slip right up next to him. I looked him in the eye and he looked back at this tall, skinny girl who had asked him for an autograph. I am sure he would have signed one for me, but I didn't have any paper or anything for him to write with. It was somewhat embarrassing, but it made him smile.

I never liked school, but my grades were good and I worked on the newspaper at Vashon High School. History was my favorite subject, but even back then I questioned how it was written. It was all this talk about freedom, but it didn't mean anything because it just wasn't true. We had segregated movies, segregated schools, hotels, and neighborhoods. Everything was segregated.

Before I graduated, my father died in 1950 of pneumonia. He was a diabetic. He went to work one Friday, came home that night, and didn't get out of bed the next two days. We took him to the doctor early Monday and he died that night. He was forty-eight years old.

After the funeral, we moved to the west end of town, into a two-story, red-brick house on Ridge Street. I needed to get a job and so I did—at Citron's drugstore in Clayton, a high-class white suburb. I worked at the soda fountain. My sister Martha worked there, too. I enrolled at Harris Stowe Teachers College, though I wasn't too crazy about the idea of becoming a teacher. In those days, teachers were not allowed to get married. Like most girls, I wanted a wedding ring.

My father was always very protective of his girls, and back then we were known as the Henley sisters. We became very popular with the boys. Martha had many boyfriends, but she settled down and married a nice young man named Moses Hart in 1950. They are still married today. Loyette had her boyfriends, too, and she made her money working as the regular babysitter for the Reverend Carroll Chambliss. He was a navy chaplain who moved into our neighborhood shortly after the war. Years later his son, Chris, would play first base for the New York Yankees.

I had my share of suitors, boyfriends who for the most part were what I would call "jive cats." You couldn't take them seriously. Then one night in the fall of 1953 I met someone different. His name was Elston Howard.

CHAPTER TWO

Emmaline's Son

I remember giving him his first write-up as a sandlotter. He so impressed me that I predicted by the time he reached twenty-one years of age, he would be in the big leagues.
—TWEED WEBB, *ST. LOUIS ARGUS*

IN 1928, A YOUNG SCHOOLTEACHER NAMED EMMALINE WEBB CAME TO St. Louis to have her baby. She arrived during the Christmas season with a broken heart. A young, handsome educator named Travis Howard was responsible for that. What once was a sweet romance had turned sour when she became pregnant while teaching grade school in Sikeston, Missouri, a small town about 180 miles south of St. Louis.

Travis Howard was a man who believed in education. It was his life. Born in 1898, he grew up in a well-to-do family in Memphis. A tall, slender man, he dressed smartly in conservative suits and knew how to talk and not sound like a preacher. He was a Tuskegee University scholar; as a student, he had lived next door to George Washington Carver. He came to Sikeston in the aftermath of a terrible incident in which three black people were killed by an angry white mob. Some things are not to be forgotten, Travis believed. Lynching is to blacks like the Holocaust is to Jews. Travis came to Sikeston intent on building a school for black children. In the years to come he would build his school in a town he could call his own. In 1953 he founded a town and named it after himself. To this day it is still called Howardsville.

As principal at the O'Bannon School, he charmed a young teacher from Arkansas, and she became pregnant. When she told him the news, he backed away. Marriage to Emmaline Webb, as he saw it, was out of the question. Child support? Not if your name was Travis Howard. She was not good enough, his family said. Rumors sprang up; they said Emmaline was messing around with other men.

Emmaline's parents had moved to St. Louis from Arkansas. Her brother, Marshall, lived there, too. They made her feel at home. On February 23, 1929, Emmaline gave birth to a healthy boy. She named him Elston. His last name would be Howard, because she knew who the father was. She could see it every time she looked into her son's big brown eyes.

For the first few years, Elston grew up in the care of his grandparents. By the time he was five, Emmaline had found a steady job as a dietitian at Peoples' Hospital and had married a steelworker named Wayman Hill, a stout, soft-spoken man who worked at the Missouri Rolling Mills Steel foundry. Young Elston called him "Big Poppy."

With Elston in tow, the Hills settled into a four-room house at 3212 Chouteau Street, right next to the house occupied by Emmaline's brother. It was a flat tenement house that overlooked the Compton Avenue Bridge, which spanned a series of railroad tracks flanked by a number of markets and industrial sites. Right across the street was an old roundhouse filled with dozens of dirt-stained railroad cars.

Emmaline was a churchgoing woman. Every Sunday she took her son to the Mt. Zion Baptist Church on Papin Street. In 1935 the Reverend Jeremiah M. Baker, a dynamic young minister, became the eleventh pastor in the church's proud seventy-six-year history. When Elston was baptized, Reverend Baker became Elston's godfather.

To Elston, Baker became an important father figure, more so than Wayman Hill and his uncle, Marshall. Young Elston spent hours helping out at the church, and Reverend Baker took a strong interest in his well-being. With Reverend Baker's help, Elston by age thirteen had landed a part-time job at Bauer's grocery store on LaSalle Street. Sometimes Elston could earn up to a dollar a day delivering groceries and doing odd chores. By the time he was sixteen, he was a weekend store clerk. At Bauer's, live chickens were cooped up outside the front door. When customers picked out their chickens, it was Elston's job to take them inside, wring their necks, and then pluck them. He hated that job.

Like most black kids on the south side, he attended grade school at 2612 Papin Street. The school, named after the Haitian slave revolt leader Toussaint L'Ouverture, was built on the site of Reverend Baker's old church. At L'Ouverture, Elston was a bright, attentive student with a knack for mathematics. In seventh grade he had a teacher named Myrtle McKinney. In those days, teachers were somewhat like priests: If you got married, you lost your job. Ms. McKinney was a big, matronly woman who was very strict in her classroom, but she loved baseball. Elston was bigger than most twelve-year-olds, and she took particular note of his baseball prowess in the schoolyard. When she saw how far Elston could hit the ball, she promised him a quarter every time he hit one over the fence.

There was nothing Elston liked more than playing ball and hanging out with his friends. When he and his buddies had no ball, they would take a broom and play with bottlecaps. Indian ball, cart ball; you name it, they played it. He was pretty good at basketball as well, developing a good one-handed set shot at the nearby Buder Community Center playground. Elston also loved to chase rabbits and got pretty good at running them down. If you couldn't sell them, you could always eat them. Elston loved hunting. One of his most prized Christmas gifts was a BB gun given to him by Big Poppy.

Elston rarely got into trouble. One day when he was about twelve, he and Fred Jones, one of his friends who lived around the corner, both got whippings when Fred killed one of the neighbor's chickens. Around Compton Hill, stealing was a common occurrence. Henry Wise, the white man who owned a corner market on Compton Avenue, was a frequent target. Maybe that's why it was said he hated black kids so much. You could buy a pint of ice cream for a dime, but he'd throw it at you.

Compton Hill had its share of black gangs, notably the Comrades and Barricudas. Elston was told to steer clear of them. He had a good sense of right and wrong. He'd always be home by nine o'clock when the whistle blew at the nearby Liggett and Myers cigarette factory. As a teenager, when several of his buddies were taking their first sips of wine, Elston had soda pop. When they were eating candy bars, Elston was eating grapes. Being a dietitian, his mother always insisted that her son eat right. She was a health nut who owned all sorts of books, including one about smoking that displayed graphic pictures of what tobacco use could do to your lungs.

When it came to girls, Elston was a mama's boy. In fact, she taught him how to dance. He was shy and rarely hung out on the street or went to school dances. His good friend Wendell Hill tried to get his sister to teach Elston how to dance for the school prom. Maybe he was reluctant to dance because of his big feet; by the time he was fifteen, he was wearing size-thirteen shoes. His friends began calling him "Foots."

In the summer of 1945, Elston was playing ball at the field they called the Dust Bowl, a large sandlot at the corner of Market and Grand, when he was spotted by a man waiting for a streetcar. The biggest kid on the field was hitting the ball so hard and so far that it made the man mad. He thought this kid was too big to be playing with kids so much smaller, and went over to tell him so. When he got to the field, he found out that the big kid was, in fact, one of the youngest on the lot. That's how Teannie Edwards met Elston Howard.

No one in St. Louis knew more about baseball than Frank Tetenus Edwards. Born in 1905, he grew up in Mill Creek, the poorest section of St. Louis, where he played ball and watched the St. Louis Stars, the local black team that competed in the Negro Leagues. The Stars played their games at the Dust Bowl. At five-feet, eight inches, Edwards was a scrappy shortstop who played in the late '20s for a barnstorming semipro team called the Tennessee Rats. He returned to St. Louis in 1931, but soon left to play in the Negro Leagues with the Cincinnati Tigers, the St. Louis Stars, and later, in 1939, the storied Homestead Grays, where he was a teammate of Josh Gibson and Buck Leonard. Teannie called Josh Gibson the "greatest hitter I ever saw." In later years, Teannie would show off a newspaper clipping of the time Josh hit a ball 513 feet in a game at Monessen, Pennsylvania.

In the days before Jackie Robinson, there was something magical about baseball in St. Louis. Until they folded in 1939, the St. Louis Stars were a competitive team. Hundreds of fans would come to the Dust Bowl to see Cool Papa Bell and Luke Easter, two of the hometown favorites. Of course, there were the white teams, the American League Browns and the Gas House Gang Cardinals, but you had to sit in the colored-only section. The Browns had theirs in left field; the Cardinals' was in right.

In 1941, when Teannie's playing days were over, he returned to St. Louis, married, and spent the war years as a packer at Wagner Electric. After the war he founded and managed a semipro team that he called the St. Louis Braves. The Braves played in the Rube Foster League, which, according to *St. Louis Argus* sportswriter Tweed Webb, was founded on March 25, 1946, by Teannie, Chink McDonald, Fay Robinson, Branch Edwards, and Ben Williams.

The Braves traveled to nearby towns and played games where, sometimes, they would pass the hat among the crowd, earning five to seven dollars per player per game. Often they would play on Sundays at Tandy Park on the west end of town, where scores of people would come out and watch them while sitting on soda crates.

When Teannie saw how far Elston could hit a baseball, he knew he had himself a ballplayer. Teannie wanted Elston on his team, but Elston was only sixteen years old and had to convince Emmaline, who wasn't so sure. She wanted her son to be a doctor, not a ballplayer. Furthermore, Emmaline didn't want her son going away on road trips and eating bad food like baloney and crackers. Teannie had to assure her that he would keep an eye on Elston and make sure he ate "special food." When it came to Elston, Teannie always made sure that Emmaline's son kept his "shirt on right." When his daughter Gloria began making eyes at his star ballplayer, Teannie put an end to it right away. "I don't want that boy distracted," he said.

Teannie was an excellent baseball teacher who stressed fundamentals. Quickly finding out that Elston had good baseball smarts, he made him a catcher. He didn't have to tinker with Elston's batting stance. Elston had a closed stance and when he cocked the bat back, he would hold his hands high, enabling him to take mighty cuts at the ball. Teannie loved Elston's versatility: Elston could play first base, outfield, anywhere but pitcher. On April 21, 1946, an Easter Sunday, Elston made his Tandy

League debut as a catcher in a game against a local team from Kinloch. He had two hits and threw out two runners in a 5–4 loss.

Teannie was a shrewd man and a strict disciplinarian. Mental mistakes were intolerable to him. If an outfielder threw to the wrong base, he'd chew him out, maybe even pull him out of the game. Teannie preached the three Rs—respect, restraint, and responsibility. "Do your job, do it well, and keep your mouth shut," that was Teannie's credo.

Elston was eighteen years old and working at Bauer's the day he heard the news on the radio about Jackie Robinson. In 1947, if you were young, black, and loved baseball, there was no better news. Even in St. Louis, they were dancing in the streets. Suddenly everyone wanted to become the next Jackie Robinson.

Vashon High School, one of the two black high schools in St. Louis, didn't have a baseball team in 1946, but after Jackie Robinson's big-league success, they had no choice but to field one. E. G. Mosely, the school's principal, called phys-ed teacher Clement Sutton into his office and told him he was going to be the baseball coach. "Get out there and work with these kids," Mosely told him. "You don't know when you might discover the next Jackie Robinson."

As a junior, Elston emerged as one of the school's top athletes. He played two seasons on the football team, handling kickoffs and punts and using his big, sure hands to catch passes as an end for Vashon's single-wing offense. "Whenever I hear stories that Elston Howard was a slow runner, I have to laugh because obviously they never had to tackle him," says Don Motley, a player for a rival high school who is now the head man at the Negro League Baseball Hall of Fame in Kansas City. "Not only was he big, but he was fast."

Naturally, Elston also distinguished himself in track as a quarter-miler, running on the relay team and setting a state record in the shot put. He played center for the basketball team, averaging twenty points a game, and was named all-state. "Elston was the finest basketball player around at the time and I still think basketball was his finest sport," said Jody Bailey, Vashon's legendary basketball coach, in 1962. "I believe he was the first boy in this area to come up with a jump shot. You couldn't stop his jump shot easily. We won twenty-seven out of twenty-eight games each of the two years he was on the team."

Elston was the best player on Vashon's new baseball team. Because they could play only black schools, they scheduled just eight games a season. "Elston looked like a big-leaguer the first day he reported to me," Sutton recalled in 1962. "He had a good arm and he could hit."

After Elston had graduated from Vashon, he spent the summer playing for the Braves. When the St. Louis Cardinals announced they were holding a four-day tryout, Teannie persuaded Elston and Wendell Hill to go Sportsman's Park and give it a go. There were three other black players among the one hundred or so who turned out, but Elston was the best. "I did as good as anybody else at the tryout," Elston recalled in 1964. "I pumped about three of them out of the park and I made it to the final day of the tryout, then they said they'd send me a letter."

Robert L. Burnes, a sportswriter for the *St. Louis Globe-Democrat*, saw Elston that day at the tryout. In 1980, he wrote an article about a lunch he had with Cardinals scout George Sisler Jr., son of the St. Louis Browns hall of famer, who also was impressed by Elston's talent. "I've been watching the best young prospect I've looked at in a year," Sisler told Joe Monahan, the head of the Cardinals' farm system. "A big, good-looking kid, just out of Vashon High School. He lives in St. Louis. I worked him out for two days, and I'd stake my job on his ability to make it."

Elston would have signed with the Cardinals, but he never heard back from them. They were not ready to sign any black players. They didn't bring up their first black player until Tom Alston made it in 1954.

In the spring of 1948, Elston had scholarship offers from several colleges. Three Big Ten schools—Illinois, Michigan, and Michigan State—recruited him for football. Nine schools wanted him for baseball, basketball, or track. That summer, Teannie saw something in Elston that he did not like. Elston seemed more interested in hanging out with his friends than in playing baseball. Elston loved pinball machines almost as much as shooting pool and he was seen frequently at the billiard hall on Rutgers Street. Teannie knew something was up one day when he came to pick Elston up for practice and found him in the pool hall, hiding under one of the tables. Even worse, sometimes he'd find Elston sneaking off to the sandlot to play softball. "Softball and baseball don't mix," Teannie later recalled in a 1962 newspaper interview. "So I had to get him out of town." Teannie called his friend William Dismukes, the head scout of the Kansas City Monarchs, and invited him to see the Braves play a Sunday doubleheader against another local team known as the Kinloch Grays. "The boy's a natural," Teannie told him. Dismukes came to St. Louis with his friend Quincy Troupe, and they were impressed, enough so that Dismukes, Troupe, and Teannie went to Emmaline's house that very evening in an attempt to sign Elston to a professional baseball contract. Once again, Emmaline needed to be convinced. Elston was in the next room, listening to the whole conversation. Teannie explained what he had in mind, but Emmaline kept expressing her wish to see her boy become a doctor. Elston began to cry, and his mother heard him. She called him into the room.

"What do you want to do?" she asked her son.

"Mama, I want to play ball," he said.

Emmaline looked to Teannie. "I always trusted your judgment. If you think he's good enough . . ."

Moments later, Elston's name was on a baseball contract. He was about to join the Kansas City Monarchs, the same team that Jackie Robinson had played for before he signed with the Brooklyn Dodgers. Elston's paycheck, about five hundred dollars a month, it was agreed, would be sent home to Emmaline.

That night, the boy they called Foots was packing his bags for Kansas City.

CHAPTER THREE

Kansas City

*Elston could handle anything that came his way. He and I just
wanted to play in the major leagues and we had to carry ourselves in
the right manner. We had to be impeccable on and off the field.*
                                                    —ERNIE BANKS

NO TOWN IN THE MIDWEST WAS QUITE LIKE KANSAS CITY. ELSTON
Howard was nineteen years old when William Dismukes brought him
there in the summer of 1948, and the years he spent there were good ones.

Elston eventually came to realize that playing in Kansas City was
indeed something special. Playing for the Monarchs, he would later say,
was a lot like playing for the New York Yankees. He played with and
against the best baseball players, stayed in all the good hotels, ate in the
best restaurants, and heard the best music in the world. To Elston, Kansas
City revolved around Eighteenth and Vine Streets, on the east side of
town, not too far from Ruppert Field at Twenty-second and Brooklyn.
Like many of the Monarchs, Elston took a room at the Streets Hotel and
was treated liked royalty. The Streets Hotel was the place to stay. It was a
three-story, red-bricked building with a barber shop and a big restaurant
called the Rose Room on the first floor. The Streets was located in the
heart of the black commercial district, on Eighteenth Street, just around
the corner from the Booker T. Hotel, near the building on Paseo Street
where Rube Foster had founded the Negro Leagues in 1920.

Everything a good-looking young man like Elston could ask for was within his reach. When he wanted to eat, he could order a big plate of eggs, bacon, grits, and toast for thirty-five cents at the Rose Room. A big, juicy Kansas City steak dinner with all the trimmings could be had for a dollar and two cents tax. Elston used to call it a "dollar-two." Legendary barbecue restaurateur Arthur Bryant was a big baseball fan who was delighted whenever the Monarchs players would stop by his rib joint at the corner of Eighteenth and Brooklyn. Elston could go there and eat all the ribs he wanted—often free of charge.

With his five-hundred-dollar monthly salary, Elston developed an affinity for buying clothes. There was no need to go downtown, where the white merchants would not allow black people to try on clothing. If you tried it on downtown, you bought it. Instead, he went to Myers Tailor Shop. That's where Buck O'Neil got his clothes. In 1948, Buck was the thirty-seven-year-old player-manager of the Monarchs, and he always dressed impeccably. Hickey Freeman suits, sweaters, slacks, argyle socks; that was Buck.

Buck had a very good team when Elston arrived that summer. Buck himself was still playing some first base; the rest of the infield featured Herb Souell at third, Hank Thompson and Curtis Roberts at second, and Gene Baker at shortstop. The outfield was solid with Bob Thurman, Johnny Scott, Willard Brown, and Curtis Roberts. On the pitching staff were Gene Collins, Ford Smith, Frank Barnes, Jim LaMarque, Booker McDaniels, and Gene Richardson.

Attendance at Monarchs games was good; they could draw up to eleven thousand fans, though there was concern that the league itself was beginning to die in the wake of Jackie Robinson's breaking of the color barrier. In 1929, the Monarchs had been the first team to install lights for night games. The major leagues didn't have lights until 1935. Kansas City was the dominant team in the Negro American League, founded in 1937. Monarch home games were an event. Fans from all over the Midwest, even white people, would dress up in their Sunday best to see the Monarchs, who played as many as twenty home games and dozens more all over the country. Many fans came to see who the next Jackie Robinson would be. Jackie had played for the Monarchs in 1945, and Elston and many of his teammates were determined to follow in Robinson's footsteps.

Elston knew all about the Negro Leagues when he got to Kansas City in July. He was always an avid reader of newspapers. His favorite sportswriter was Tweed Webb. Tweed was the sports authority of black St. Louis, and his articles in the weekly St. Louis Argus documented the talents of local black athletes such as Luke Easter and Cool Papa Bell as well as other Negro League greats such as Josh Gibson, Buck Leonard and, of course, Satchel Paige.

For years, Tweed Webb had championed the St. Louis Stars. When they folded in 1939, Webb frequently wrote about the Kansas City Monarchs, who played many of their away games in towns in and around St. Louis. To play for the Monarchs, Webb wrote, you had to be the best. Hundreds of kids like Elston learned all about the great Monarchs teams of the early '40s that included Paige, Hank Thompson, and Willard Brown. When Jackie broke the color barrier, all three of those players quickly followed him into the majors, where they played for the St. Louis Browns. That left it up to Dismukes to replenish the Monarchs with suitable talent wherever he could find it. Dismukes himself was a Negro League pitcher who was the team's traveling secretary and chief scout.

When Dismukes showed up with Elston, Buck took an instant liking to his new player. In Elston he had a model citizen, a smart young player who would never stay out at night, wouldn't get drunk or chase after women. "Shoot, I never had to worry about Elston off the field," Buck would later say. "He was a fine young man. With Elston it was always baseball, baseball, baseball. He had big hands, he could throw the ball, had some pop in his bat. He wanted to play. All of the guys liked him. In my book, he was a couldn't miss."

Buck already had a good dependable catcher in another St. Louis product, Earl "Mickey" Taborn, so he played Elston in left field. Whenever Buck didn't feel like playing first base, he put Elston there. In Elston's first game at Ruppert Stadium, it is said he hit one over the scoreboard in left center field. "I got one of my first big thrills that first year with the Monarchs," Elston recalled in 1963. "One day I hit three homers and the next day two more." Teammates liked Elston, too. Elston and

Mickey Taborn became roommates. Connie Johnson and Frank Barnes became his big brothers. Elston used to call Johnson "Greasy." He would knock on Johnson's door and say, "C'mon, Greasy, let's go eat." Greasy and Barnes showed him around town; they teased him about his shoe size, played cards, took him to movies, and showed him the nightclubs.

Elston loved music—big band, blues, swing, jazz—and he was in the perfect place to hear it all. All the top musicians, including Count Basie, Charlie Parker, Julia Lee, Jay McShann, Joe Turner, Pearl Bailey, and Sarah Vaughn, brought their sounds of magic into joints like the Blue Room and Reno Club. Count Basie came to Kansas City so much he named his band the KC 7. "All the ballplayers wanted to be musicians and all the musicians wanted to be ballplayers," recalled Buck, who used to let Lionel Hampton coach first base during Monarch games. Later, when Elston played for the Yankees, Hampton always invited him to his shows at the Starlight Room whenever he came to New York.

Elston loved playing with the Monarchs despite an arduous travel schedule that saw them play night after night in city after city. He loved baseball so much, he didn't mind the all-night bus rides. According to some records, he batted .283 for the Monarchs in 1948. The season ended when they lost to the Birmingham Barons—a team that featured a young Willie Mays—in the playoffs. Elston hit .270 in 1949. In 1950 Taborn left the Monarchs for Newark and Elston got a new roommate. His name was Ernie Banks.

"I can still see his smile," Banks would say later. "He smiled a lot. We talked a lot. We did everything together. We went to the movies, the park, shared the same seats on trips, ate together in restaurants. He had more experience than I did. I would follow his lead. Wherever he would go, I would go. We talked about everything. We became brothers. He was two years older than me. Yeah, and we talked about getting married. I had no girlfriend at the time, and I don't think he did either."

But Elston did have a girlfriend. Her name was Delores Williams, and she lived in Compton Hill, on Caroline Street. She was Elston's high school sweetheart. They used to hang out outside Chitney's Sandwich Shop on Hickory Street. She was studying to be a nurse at Homer Phillips, the black public hospital in St. Louis. While Elston was in Kansas

City for the 1950 season, he wrote her letters and saw her whenever he went home. One night the Monarchs were in St. Louis and some of the players went to eat dinner at the Majestic Restaurant. Elston brought Delores and introduced her to Buck. "She was very nice," Buck recalled. "He brought her up to me and said, 'Buck, I want you to meet my girl.'"

Elston and Ernie dreamed of making it to the major leagues, and they made a little bet that spring. Whoever made it first would have to call the other and tell what it was like.

Tom Baird, the white owner of the Monarchs, soon came to realize that there was a lot of money to be made by selling his players to the major-league teams. He wanted to be a Yankee farm team. Dozens of major-league scouts flocked to Kansas City to check out the talent at Monarch games, even Tom Greenwade, one of the top Yankee scouts, the man who had discovered and signed Mickey Mantle. In 1950 the Yankees had very few black players in their farm system, and they needed to keep pace with other teams—notably the Dodgers and Giants—who were signing blacks by the dozens. The Boston Braves were interested in Elston, but with the Korean War flaring up, they decided not to invest in a young player who might be drafted into the army. The Cincinnati Reds sent a scout to look at him, but Buck O'Neil had another team in mind for his young star. Buck liked Elston's work ethic and attitude. "He was a professional ballplayer," Buck would say. "I wanted the Yankees to have a black ballplayer and I knew Elston was the type of player they were looking for." When Greenwade arrived to check out Willard Brown, who had returned to the Monarchs from the St. Louis Browns, Buck pointed directly toward Elston. "Willard's a fine player," Buck told Greenwade, "but the boy you're looking for is right over there. Elston Howard is the player you're looking for." A few days later, Tom Baird happily signed over the papers that would send Elston and Frank Barnes to the Yankee organization for twenty-five thousand dollars. Later that season, Baird also sold Bob Thurman to the Yankees.

The Yankees told Elston, then twenty-one years old, that he would go to their Class A team in Muskegon, Michigan. "I was frightened by the publicity I got," Elston recalled. "The first Negro player on the Yankee club. That's what they said I was going to be."

The Muskegon team was managed by Bob Finley. When Elston got there on July 26, the Clippers had a 39–46 record and were sixteen games out of first place in the eight-team Central League. An article in the *Sporting News* reported that Elston made a "good impression" in his debut that day. Starting in left field, he had a single in four at-bats and threw out a runner by twelve feet at the plate. On August 4, Elston, paid four hundred dollars a month, homered and doubled, and the Clippers began to rise in the standings. Elston played fifty-four games for the Clippers and batted .283 with nine homers and 42 RBIs. In those games, the Clippers were 36–18 to finish the regular season at 75–64, good enough for second place, eight games behind Flint. In the playoffs, Elston continued to lead the way. Batting cleanup, he had five hits as the Clippers needed four games to eliminate Dayton in a best-of-five series. In the Central League finals, they lost to Flint in five games. The only Clipper highlight came in Game 3 when Elston homered in the sixth inning of an 11–0 win.

The season ended, and Elston went home to St. Louis. When he got home Delores was waiting for him. Elston called Ernie Banks to tell him they had decided to get married. Just before the wedding, Elston got a letter telling him he was being inducted into the army. The Korean War was under way. The Yankees had assigned him to their Class AA team in Binghamton, New York, but that was going to have to wait. Elston was in camp when his brief marriage ended in divorce. There are conflicting stories about what happened. One story has it that Delores's parents didn't approve of her marrying a ballplayer and annulled the marriage. Another story said she fell in love with a postal worker named James Griffin and told Elston she didn't love him anymore. A third story claims that Elston only married Delores because she claimed to be pregnant. When he found out she was not pregnant, he had the marriage annulled.

The army sent Elston to Jefferson Barracks in St. Louis. When they found out how good a baseball player he was, he was stationed at Fort Leonard Wood in central Missouri before being assigned to special services and sent to Japan. Elston never saw a minute of combat. All his commanding officer ever asked was that he play baseball for the base team. Elston was serving his country by playing the game he loved. How sad. He should have been playing in the major leagues.

CHAPTER FOUR

The Wedding

You know what they said about Elston: He only had two girlfriends and he married both of them.

—BUCK O'NEILL

EVERYONE IN ST. LOUIS KNEW ABOUT ELSTON HOWARD. I KNEW HE WAS a good baseball player. I read the stories in the newspaper. I knew he was doing something with his life. My sister Martha knew him from Vashon. They had been in the same classes together, but because he was a big-time jock, they hung out with different crowds. I never met Elston until one night when Loyette and I went to the Riviera Club on Delmar Street.

Elston was out of the army and had finished playing the 1953 season with the Yankees' top minor-league team, the Kansas City Blues. He came to the Riviera Club that night with his friend Wendell Hill. Wendell supposedly suggested to Elston that he go over and talk to Loyette. He did, but he talked to me, too. Right away I could see he was shy and very polite; I liked that. There was something serious about him; he was very conservative and well mannered. I liked that, too. He was such a gentleman, very tall, very handsome. He and Wendell offered to escort us home, and we accepted the offer. Elston had a car; that was impressive, even though it turned out that it belonged to Elston's godfather, Reverend Baker. I sat in the back seat while Loyette sat up front with Elston. The next day, Elston called me, not Loyette, on the phone and asked me out. I don't think Loyette ever forgave me for that.

Elston and I began dating that fall, and things quickly got serious. For the first time in my life, I was in love, and it didn't take long before we were talking marriage. One night, just before Christmas, we were in my mother's living room when Elston got down on his knees and asked me to marry him. Naturally, I said yes. At first, my mother wasn't happy about our engagement because Elston had not asked her permission to marry me. Elston blamed me for that, because I had told him I thought it was old-fashioned to ask for your parents' permission to get married.

When he went to play for the Toronto Maple Leafs in the spring of 1954, Elston phoned me whenever he could and wrote me a letter every day. Usually he wrote about how much he missed me, what his batting average was, and the things he did and cities he saw. That summer, I took a vacation and went to visit him while the Maple Leafs played a series in Syracuse. When he returned home in September, he brought me a big engagement ring. I was so thrilled. We were going to be married, and we began making plans for a church wedding that spring.

That fall, there were stories in the newspapers around town that Elston would be playing the 1955 season with the New York Yankees. One day, his mother got a surprising phone call. It was Travis Howard. He had seen one of the articles and now, all of a sudden, he had decided to come to St. Louis to meet his son. What gall! Elston did not want to see him. He wanted nothing to do with the man who had deemed his mother not worthy of marrying. But Elston's mother persuaded him to meet with Travis. There was a lot of tension that day. I was there with Elston when he met his father for the first time. When we arrived at Emmaline's house on St. Louis Avenue, Travis was sitting in the living room, in a big chair. He had the same features as Elston, the same type of head and face, even the big feet. The only notable difference was that he was bald.

Elston nervously shook hands with his father, who immediately began making apologies. When Elston introduced me as his fiancée, Travis began asking questions about me and my background, even though he didn't know anything about his son. All he knew was that Elston was going to be playing baseball for the New York Yankees. Emmaline was very happy about the whole thing. She was so proud. She felt vindicated. She knew she had raised a successful son.

Elston asked Travis for money. Elston had an attitude and felt his father owed him something. His attitude was, "You never gave me anything and you're doing OK and I need a car." Travis gave him one hundred dollars or so, and it helped Elston to buy his first car, a brown and yellow Pontiac.

We were going to invite Travis to the wedding, but all our plans changed just after Thanksgiving when the Yankees called. They told Elston they wanted him to play winter ball in Puerto Rico. The spring wedding was off. Right then, we decided to get married as soon as we could. And so we did, on December 4, 1954, in my mother's living room. Reverend Baker performed the ceremony. Loyette was the maid of honor, and my brother Nathaniel was Elston's best man. Travis didn't come.

We spent our honeymoon in Puerto Rico. We got an apartment in San Juan, in the same complex with several other American ballplayers, notably George Crowe, Sam Jones, and Willie Mays. They were our neighbors. Living in San Juan that winter was a lot of fun. We had a few parties and a couple of cookouts. We had quite a social club.

George Crowe and his wife, Yvonne, became two of our best friends. They came with their two daughters. George, who played for San Juan's rival team, Santuce, always liked Elston and constantly gave him words of encouragement. "You're with the right team," George told him. "Yogi's on the way out."

By late February, it was time to pack up and head for home. Elston was going to spring training in St. Petersburg, Florida. I went home to St. Louis, knowing I was pregnant. My life would never be same.

CHAPTER FIVE

The White Yankees

The Yankees will bring up a Negro as soon as one that fits the high Yankee standards is found.
—Yankees general manager George Weiss

It's no secret that Jackie Robinson hated the New York Yankees. The sting of four World Series losses was not the only reason why he despised the so-called Bronx Bombers. After Jackie broke the color barrier in 1947, the Yankees continued to dominate the Brooklyn Dodgers and the rest of the major leagues with all-white lineups. On November 30, 1952, on a New York TV show called *Youth Wants to Know*, Jackie Robinson blasted baseball's most prominent team. A young girl asked Jackie why the Yankees had no black ballplayers. Without blinking, he said, "I think the Yankee management is prejudiced."

Robinson's comment wasn't the first shot taken at the Yankees. On April 15, 1952, a group called the American Labor Party set up picket lines outside Yankee Stadium. The pickets, mostly white and accused of being communists by some, issued leaflets condemning the Yankees for being "the only lily-white team left in New York."

George Weiss, the longtime Yankee general manager, saw no need to integrate a ball club strongly supported by white, upscale fans. Economically, the Yankees had no use for black players, especially since the New York Black Yankees continued to attract a hearty share of their own fans in the Negro National League. Plus the Black Yankees had to pay the

Yankees rent to use their stadium, where they would on occasion draw crowds of up to thirty thousand.

Weiss, once described by *New York Post* columnist Jimmy Cannon as "a dour man with the cold serenity of a pawnbroker," was blinded by Yankee success, not to mention a deep-rooted prejudice against black people. "I will never allow a black man to wear a Yankee uniform," he declared at a cocktail party in 1952. "Boxholders from Westchester don't want them. They would be offended to have to sit with niggers."

It took until 1950, three years after Robinson had arrived in the majors, for the George Weiss Yankees to sign their first black ballplayers. Yet two years later there were still no blacks on the Yankee major-league roster. "Robinson's remarks are shocking," Weiss said in rebuttal to Robinson's comments, "because he, like any person connected with baseball, must know of the efforts we have made to find Negro players of major-league ability. Our efforts in that respect are well known." Weiss added that "with the exception of Jackie Robinson we have been interested in just about every Negro player who has come up to the majors."

True, the Yankees did scout some prominent black players, but somehow Weiss and his cronies managed to overlook the extraordinary talents of Larry Doby, Luke Easter, Minnie Minoso, Monte Irvin, Roy Campanella, Don Newcombe, Sam Jethroe, and Ernie Banks. One report has it that Weiss once called Tom Greenwade, the team's leading scout, into his office and told him, "Now, Tom, we don't want you crawling through any back alleys trying to sign some niggers."

Bill McCorry was another one of Weiss's top scouts and later became the team's traveling secretary. He also was the man who overlooked Willie Mays in 1950. There's a story that McCorry went to see pitcher Bobby Shantz, who went on to star for the Philadelphia A's and other teams, including the Yankees. While scouting Shantz, McCorry also saw Mays, who was playing for the Birmingham Black Barons. McCorry, however, saw nothing in Mays to warrant recommending him to the Yankees. One year later, Mays was with the Giants. John Drebinger, a *New York Times* writer, used to needle McCorry about not signing Mays when he had the chance. Mays hit two homers one day, and Drebinger spotted McCorry and yelled out, "Hey, McCorry, two more today for Willie."

McCorry, by then the Yankee traveling secretary, turned on Drebinger. "I don't care what he did today or any other day," he told the writer. "I got no use for him or any of them. I wouldn't want any of them on a club I was with. I wouldn't arrange a berth on the train for any of them." *New York Post* columnist Milton Gross was stunned when McCorry's remark made it into print: "It would be wise to remember this though when the day arrives that the Yankees find the Negro player good enough to come up. He won't be much use on the road without a proper place to sleep."

In 1950, the Yankees were involved in a dispute with Cleveland Indians owner Bill Veeck over the signing of a Puerto Rican outfielder named Luis Marquez. Baseball commissioner Happy Chandler was called in; he awarded Marquez to the Indians and sent a thirty-year-old black shortstop named Artie Wilson to the Yankees. Weiss wasn't happy with the decision, and Wilson was released soon after. Wilson had twenty-two at-bats with the New York Giants in 1951 and was never heard from again. Marquez surfaced in the majors in 1951, lasting two seasons with the Boston Braves, Chicago Cubs, and Pittsburgh Pirates.

Although Weiss maintained otherwise, the Yankees seemed intent on remaining an all-white team. It didn't help that they were managed by Casey Stengel. The crusty old Yankee manager made no secret of his dislike for Robinson, who often was the subject of catcalls and bench-jockeying from the Yankee bench during World Series games. Stengel's animosity toward the Dodger star probably was more a case of professional jealousy than absolute bigotry. Stengel had no player who could match Robinson's supreme baserunning talent. Robinson would take great delight in running wild against Casey's Yankees. Stengel once warned his players, "You better look in your lockers and make sure he didn't steal your jockstraps." After Allie Reynolds, who was part Creek Indian, struck out Robinson three times in the 1952 World Series, Stengel barked out: "Before that black son of a bitch accuses us of being prejudiced, he should learn how to hit an Indian." Whenever he got the chance, Robinson dared the Yankees to prove him a liar, and he never took back his remarks. Six seasons had passed since he had broken baseball's color barrier, and the Yankees had five straight World Series titles and zero blacks on their major-league roster.

In the early 1950s, the Yankee farm system had a few promising black players. There was Bob Thurman, a pitcher-outfielder who had hit tape-measure home runs for the Homestead Grays and the Kansas City Monarchs. Thurman was signed by the Yankees in 1950, an event his wife years later called "a publicity stunt." Thurman and Mickey Taborn, Elston's old roommate on the Monarchs, played for the Triple-A Newark Bears. Taborn was traded off to the Cubs along with another black infielder named Frank Austin. Thurman eventually surfaced in the majors as a thirty-four-year-old rookie in 1955 with the Cincinnati Reds. Austin never made it to the big leagues.

Then there was Vic Power. He had the talent to be the first black Yankee, but the flashy Puerto Rico–born first baseman with the quick bat was traded to the Philadelphia Athletics after the 1953 season in an eleven-player deal. Power, a notorious bad-ball hitter and slick fielder with an attitude, obviously was not in the Yankee mold. It is generally believed the Yankees wanted no part of Power because he was said to be dating a white woman in Kansas City. In truth, according to Buck O'Neil, she was a light-skinned black woman.

In 1953, Vic Power and Elston Howard were teammates at the Yankees' top farm team, Kansas City. Although Power had a .349 batting average, better than Elston's .286, Weiss and the Yankee front office claimed that Power had not hustled. "They were just looking for excuses," Power said. "What did they want me to do? Mow the lawn in the outfield, too?" Power went to the A's, and eventually won six Gold Gloves and batted over .300 three times in his career. When it came to racism, Power always tried to make fun of it. One story has it that he once got arrested in the South, allegedly for jaywalking. "I thought the 'Don't Walk' sign was for whites only," he told the judge, tongue firmly in cheek.

"He never knew when to keep his mouth shut," recalls Andy Carey, the Yankee third baseman who played with Power in the late '50s. "He was the only player who if he was in a fight, nobody would want to help. He was his own worst enemy. He could hit, he was fancy with the glove, but, boy, did he have a way of antagonizing you."

After Power was traded away, Elston began to get more attention. "Howard is faster afoot and a quicker thinker as well," Dan Daniel wrote in the *Sporting News*. "He has a better educational background." In February 1954, Elston was among the twenty-nine ballplayers who attended "Yankee Prospects School" in Lake Wales, Florida. Another black prospect at that camp was Ed "Buster" Andrews, a hard-throwing young pitcher from New Brunswick, New Jersey. Later that spring, Andrews looked impressive, throwing three scoreless innings against the Yankees in an exhibition game at Norfolk, Virginia. He held a 5–2 record at Norfolk that season, but his career abruptly ended later in the summer when he tore a tendon in his right forearm.

In Florida for Yankee spring training in 1954, Elston was hopeful. "If they send me back to Kansas City, I won't lose heart," Elston vowed. "I'll just try my best again to make it."

Jackie Robinson took note of Elston and took him aside one day. Like most black players during those days, they talked about baseball racism. Many times when black major leaguers got together, they would go up and down the roster of their teams, identifying those who would help you out and those who would call you a nigger. Jackie told Elston about his World Series experiences when Casey and the Yankees would pelt him with racial slurs from the dugout. Elston, by this point, knew the Yankee management was somewhat racist, but that was the way it was. He wanted to be a Yankee, the first black Yankee, just as Buck O'Neil had envisioned. Thousands of black American baseball fans, too, eagerly awaited the arrival of the first black Yankee. To be that person was Elston's dream. But Jackie realized Elston's job would be tough. Branch Rickey wanted and supported Jackie Robinson. Elston could never say the same thing about George Weiss.

Elston looked around the Yankee locker room and saw a room full of great players. Yogi Berra was the catcher; Mickey Mantle played center field. Hank Bauer played in right. Billy Martin was the second baseman. Phil Rizzuto, the shortstop, was asked about his first impression of Elston that spring. "He made everything he did look so easy," he said. "You could see right away he'd be around a long, long time."

"Everybody could see he was a good ballplayer," said Whitey Ford, the all-star pitcher.

"Elston had quite a presence," said Moose Skowron, a first baseman and teammate of Elston's in 1953 at Kansas City. "As big as he was, nobody was going to mess with him. He kept his mouth shut and did his job. You had to respect him."

Said infielder Jerry Coleman, "Elston was a lot better Yankee the day he joined the club than guys that were around for years."

"We had heard a lot of good things about this big kid who could hit," recalls Yogi. "We had a lot of catchers back then. He had one helluva strong arm."

Despite instant acceptance among his teammates, Elston could not stay at the team hotel. Instead, McCorry found him a room to rent from a man who ran a shoe repair stand in downtown St. Petersburg. McCorry didn't know where to go, so he just asked the first black person he knew, Bill Williams, and for years Williams and his wife would accommodate several black major leaguers and their families.

There was no guarantee Elston would make the big club that spring of 1954. His emotions remained low-key when he was told the Yankees wanted him to become a catcher, a position already ably filled by Yogi Berra. His first day at training camp, he was greeted by his former manager at Kansas City. "Bill Skiff walked over and handed me a catcher's glove. 'Here,' he said, 'get used to using this. We're going to make a catcher out of you.'" Said Stengel, "As an outfielder he would never be more than a minor leaguer. In order to play here, he'd best turn his efforts to catching."

Bill Dickey, the former Yankee Hall of Fame catcher, worked with Elston to help him develop his catching skills. Elston initially didn't like the idea, but working with Dickey was a godsend. When Dickey first saw Elston, he saw right away that he had a pupil with the tools to be a great major-league catcher: a tremendously strong throwing arm, amazing temperament, and a willingness to work hard. In Dickey, Elston saw a great teacher.

Elston never forgot the day he met Dickey. Later he would recall Dickey saying, "Howard, I see that you are ambitious. You have the desire to learn and you have the guts with which to do it. I want to help you. Place your confidence in me. You and I won't go wrong." Remembered Elston, "He was the most patient man I've ever met. All he ever wanted in return was that you pay attention and try as hard as you could. I didn't disappoint him there. I really was not much of a catcher at the start. I really wasn't much of a catcher for a good, long while, but I can honestly say I never stopped trying."

"He's a real hustler," Dickey told the press. "He wants to learn and will work all day."

Charlie Silvera, Yogi's backup, remembers that Elston was a "grabber"; Dickey made him a catcher. "You want the ball to come to you," Dickey told Elston. Thanks to Dickey's help, Elston eventually developed a style in which he would catch one-handed. As his left hand set the target, his right hand, his throwing hand, would be cocked behind his back. In his glove, Elston began using "falsies," the padding found on some women's bras, to help cushion the impact of major-league pitching.

Years later, Elston praised Dickey for molding him into a major leaguer. "Dickey made me the catcher I am," he said in 1961. "He taught me not to be afraid to get down on my knees to block a ball and how to pivot to get off my throw to second. I'm really more proud of that than anything. I'm more proud of trying hard than I am of anything. Bill Dickey taught me that—I mean to say he impressed that on me so I never forgot it."

While Dickey was working with Elston, critics lashed out at the Yankee organization once again. Was this just another poor excuse to keep Elston in the minors? The *Baltimore Afro-American* thought so. It ran a front-page story by Sam Lacy, with the headline, "Vicious Conspiracy Being Conducted." Lacy accused the Yankees of giving Elston the "runaround." "Howard . . . is so young, so trusting, so naive as to still have faith in human nature, Yankee version. If Howard is not a major leaguer as an outfielder, it stands to reason he is not a major leaguer as a catcher." In the same story, there were quotes from Elston in which he allegedly took shots at Vic Power.

When Elston heard about that story, he became enraged. "I ought to punch that guy's head off," Elston told the *New York World-Telegram* in reference to Sam Lacy. "A few weeks ago someone wrote that I said Vic Power wasn't a hustler, and things like that. I never said anything of the sort."

On March 13, 1954, Elston made his Yankee spring training debut. Catching four innings of a 4–3 win over Washington, he drove in two runs with a triple off of left-hander Dean Stewart. Elston ran so hard rounding second base that he lost his cap and didn't realize it until third-base coach Frank Crosetti pointed it out to him. "It's a thrill I'll never forget," Elston told the press afterward. "I admit I was nervous for an inning or so and I didn't feel too good when I grounded out in the third inning. Yes, sir, I certainly do feel good. Like I said at the start of spring training, I'm not claiming I'll make the club this season, but more than ever now I do feel I will get in the majors to stick."

On March 16, Elston was the catcher and had an RBI single in a 5–3 loss to Detroit. On March 22 he made his first start behind the plate, catching all nine innings and going 2-for-5 in a 12–6 win over the Philadelphia Athletics. In the first inning, Joe DeMaestri singled and tried to steal second base on the very next pitch by Eddie Lopat, but Elston nailed him with a perfect throw to second. Later on, Elston smashed a hard drive to right center, only to be robbed of an extra base hit when Vic Power, of all people, made a sensational diving catch.

By April 1, as spring camp was winding down, he had gone 6-for-17 at the plate, a batting average of .351. To some, it became obvious that Elston was good enough to play for the New York Yankees. "Some of us walked up to Casey and said, 'Hey, Case, we can use this man right now. He can help us,'" said Eddie Lopat. Then came the bad news: Elston was being sent to Lake Wales along with eight other rookies to await assignment. It was no joke. The Yankees were going north with three catchers—Yogi, Charlie Silvera, and Ralph Houk—but no Elston Howard. Somewhere in Baltimore, Sam Lacy was laughing. Reported the *Chicago Defender*, "All up and down Seventh Avenue [in Harlem] all you can hear is 'I told you so.'"

Elston could have been sent back to the top Yankee farm team in Kansas City, but because the Yankees were so inundated with catchers, they made an arrangement for Elston to play in the International League for an independent team in Toronto owned by Jack Kent Cooke. Elston became enamored with Cooke, a flashy millionaire who would later own a slew of professional teams, most notably the Los Angeles Lakers and the Washington Redskins. Elston would often phone home and tell stories about Cooke gambling his money away in Havana or sitting in the stands, showing off his beautiful blonde wife. When it came time for Elston to buy an engagement ring, Cooke sent him to his jeweler.

In Toronto, Luke Sewell, a former major-league catcher, was the manager. Elston's teammates on the Maple Leafs included pitchers Frank Barnes and Connie Johnson, two of his old teammates from the Monarchs. Another black player on the team was Sam Jethroe, a star in the Negro Leagues who was winding down his career after three productive seasons with the Boston Braves. Sewell worked Elston into the lineup every day, mostly at catcher but sometimes in center field and right field. In his first thirty-two games Elston had five home runs and 25 runs batted in. As the '54 season progressed Elston found himself in a battle for the league batting title with a young outfielder from Rochester named Bill Virdon. Virdon himself had been a Yankee prospect and a teammate of Elston's at Kansas City. But that spring he had been traded to the Cardinals' organization in a deal that included St. Louis outfielder Enos Slaughter.

On the last day of the season, Virdon went hitless and finished up at .333. Elston went 2-for-4 and finished at .331. Still, Elston won the league MVP award with 22 homers and 109 RBIs. As soon as the season ended, Elston's contract was reacquired by the Yankees and assigned to the Kansas City roster.

Meanwhile, back in New York a storm continued to brew outside Yankee Stadium. While the Dodgers and Giants were thriving at the box office with the success of their black players, another wave of demonstrations struck the big Bronx ballpark. In 1954, the Supreme Court had ruled that segregation was illegal in public schools. Integration was on the move. There were sixteen black players on six major-league baseball teams, zero with the Yankees.

In 1954, for the first time in five years, the Yankees didn't win the pennant. They won 103 games but finished in second place behind the Cleveland Indians, a team with Larry Doby in the outfield.

The Yankees were vilified by the media. Attendance was down. Elston's spirits were up. The door was wide open.

Chapter Six

The Rookie

Ellie was such a sweetheart. He put up with all that stuff and always kept his head up.

—Phil Rizzuto

In 1955, St. Petersburg, Florida, was not ready for integration. Nor was it ready for Elston Howard, and it certainly was not ready for me. Jackie Robinson was treated miserably whenever he played there during spring training. In St. Petersburg they would throw black cats on the field, yell vicious insults, and make threats against Jackie and other black ballplayers. In St. Petersburg "colored people" lived primarily on the south side of town. We had to use separate drinking fountains and bathrooms. We could not use the public beaches, except for the small "colored-only" beach near the city pier. At Webb's City, the biggest department store in town, we were not allowed to shop on two of the four floors, and certainly we were not allowed to eat at the lunch counter. At another department store, Rutland's, we were not allowed to try on clothes. On the city bus we had to sit in the back. At Al Lang Field, the local ballpark, we could only sit in the left-field bleachers. At most restaurants we could not get hamburgers unless we went around to the back. The big hotels were for "whites only."

When Elston left St. Louis for spring training that February, he knew how bad things would be. But he also knew it was the price he would have to pay to play for the New York Yankees. When Elston's train pulled into St. Pete, Bill Skowron was a familiar face waiting for him. Elston and Moose had been teammates in Kansas City in 1953. Being from Cicero, Illinois, Skowron had little experience with Jim Crow laws, so when Elston climbed into Moose's car, Skowron drove him straight to the Soreno Hotel because he didn't know better. Elston figured he would be turned away, but maybe Moose knew something he didn't; maybe this year would be different. But nothing had changed. Once again, here he was, a member of the New York Yankees, being told he could not set foot inside the hotel. Elston had to return to the Williams' boardinghouse on Fifth Avenue South. He certainly was not happy about it, but to him, it was part of the game he had to play.

Since I had just become pregnant, it was decided I would stay back in St. Louis that spring. Assuming that this time Elston was going to make the team, it was agreed that I would meet him in New York. Early in the exhibition season, the Yankees went to Miami for a series with the Dodgers. Elston couldn't stay with the team there either, so he went to a black hotel called the Sir John. Funny, but Elston never knew how to swim until he went there and used the pool. Some lifeguard taught him how. At the hotel, he ran into Jackie Robinson, Roy Campanella, Don Newcombe, and Junior Gilliam in the lobby. "Oh, you guys stay here, too?" he asked. Jackie looked up at Elston and said, "Not much longer."

Elston was confident he would make the team. There were six catchers at Miller Huggins Field, but none had his versatility. The Yankees were in need of a strong right-handed hitter and Elston, with his enormous hands and huge, powerful wrists, could catch, play left or right field, pinch-hit, and play first base. And he worked hard in practice. He would always be first up for batting practice so that he could spend the rest of the day working on his catching or shagging fly balls in the outfield.

Elston's work ethic delighted Casey Stengel, who bragged aloud frequently that spring that Elston was his "three-way man." Casey told the press that Elston would platoon with Irv Noren in left field and be the Yankees' number-one right-handed pinch-hitter. The only thing Casey didn't like about Elston was his speed. Elston wasn't a slow runner, but he was nowhere near as quick as Jackie Robinson or Willie Mays, both of whom had terrorized the Yankees in previous World Series with speed and daring on the basepaths. "When I finally get a nigger," Stengel told the press, jokingly, "I get the only one that can't run."

There really was nothing malicious about what Casey had said. If anything, Elston was upset because Casey had referred to him as a slow runner. Hey, he ran track on the relay team when he was at Vashon High School, and he led the International League with twelve triples in 1954. Even though Casey would use the "N" word and occasionally referred to Elston as "Eight Ball," Elston never really thought that Stengel was racist. Casey was just being Casey. He was sixty-five years old. That was how people of his era talked, Elston thought, and so he accepted it. Casey always was blurting out words that were unusual and embarrassing. Once, when Baltimore's Bob Boyd singled and stole a base while Elston was catching, Casey got all ticked off. When Elston got back to the dugout, Casey rushed up to Elston and said, "What pitch did that nigger hit?" Oops!

"When the game started Casey was a nervous bundle of energy," Elston recalled in a 1964 issue of *Reader's Digest*. "He used to walk up and down the dugout singing snatches of sarcastic songs at the opposing players and ending them with the same refrain, 'Tra, la, la, la la! Tra, la, la, la la!'"

Another time, Whitey Ford recalls, the Yankees brought in a scout, Rudy York was his name, to give the team a report on the Baltimore Orioles. Elston was sitting quietly in the back when York began discussing the tendencies of Connie Johnson, one of Elston's best friends when they were teammates with the Kansas City Monarchs and Toronto Maple Leafs, who was now a hard-throwing right-hander for Baltimore. "You know how niggers have white palms, right?" said the scout. "Well, if you see the whites of his palms as he delivers the ball, you know it's going to be a fastball. If you can't see them, it's a curve." Elston was embarrassed. He could have gotten angry and cursed the man out, but that was not Elston. He would never bring himself down to that level. That's not what he believed in.

Jackie Robinson was a frequent target of Stengel's dugout sniping, and he always was convinced that Casey was a racist. Elston disagreed. "I remember in the World Series he would scream at Newcombe and

Robinson and Campanella from the bench. I never heard him scream racial things. I also heard him scream at Hodges and Reese and Snider in the same way."

Casey knew Elston was going to make the team that spring, but it took a while for him to say so. "Howard's a good boy," he said, "but I can't make up my mind where he's best at, even though I've had him hittin' cleanup, which I don't do except with a real good hitter, which he is." Wrote Arthur Daley of the *New York Times*, "He seems certain to be the first Negro to make the Yankees. The men in the Yankee front office have stubbornly refused to be panicked into hiring a Negro just because he was a Negro. They've waited for one to come along who answers the description, 'the Yankee type.' Elston is a nice, quiet lad whose reserved, gentlemanly demeanor has won him complete acceptance from every Yankee."

Paul Krichell, the head scout, met Elston and gave his approval. "I like that young man," Krichell said. "Even though he's black, he has manners. The fact is any player turned loose by the Yankees was released because he didn't measure up to the requirement, and that has nothing to do with color, creed or race. Both as a man and as a ballplayer, this boy Howard looks every inch a Yankee."

Elston was twenty-six years old, and there were people around him calling him "boy." Isn't that sad?

On March 21, George Weiss made it official: Elston was going north with the team. "He has big-league talent and character," Weiss told the press. "That's the only yardstick the Yankees ever use in fielding a team." Elston's dream had come true. He was given uniform number 32, previously worn by Ralph Houk, the third-string catcher. Elston was given the standard major-league contract calling for the minimum salary of six thousand dollars. By today's standards, isn't that pitiful?

Said Charlie Silvera, "As soon as I saw Elston at spring training, I went from being the second-string catcher to the third-string catcher." Houk was sent to the minors.

Before the season opened, the Yankees left Florida for a series of exhibition games in several southern cities. The first stop was New Orleans, where "colored people" could only sit in left field. Casey decided to play Elston in right field and Hank Bauer in left. "First inning, you wouldn't believe what they called me," Elston once recalled. "So Bauer suggested we be switched. And so next inning Stengel put me over in left field with my people."

The next stop was Birmingham, Alabama, but Elston was sent ahead to Memphis because Birmingham had a city ordinance that forbid games involving white and black players. In Memphis, Elston was in uniform, but he was not allowed to take the field. Unlike the Yankees, the Dodgers and Giants knew it was smart to stay away from southern cities like these. Willie Mays was from a little town outside Birmingham, and he never wanted to play there.

When Elston got to New York, he needed an apartment. Our friend George Crowe, who was playing for the Milwaukee Braves, let us stay at his home in Springfield Gardens, Queens. Count Basie lived there, too, and we would see him all the time. Eventually, we found a nice little one-bedroom apartment on Edgecomb Avenue in upper Manhattan near the Polo Grounds. It was such a nice neighborhood, and still is today. A good number of black celebrities lived there. Joe Louis had a place he used when he couldn't get a hotel room downtown. Willie Mays lived right across the street from us, but we never saw much of him because the Giants were often on the road when the Yankees were home. Elston's cousin drove me to New York, and we arrived just before the night Elston was to appear on the *Ed Sullivan Show*. It was the Sunday night before the season opened. Everyone in St. Louis was watching on TV. Casey Stengel went on stage with his three prized rookies. And there on stage was Elston, along with pitchers Johnny Kucks and Tom Sturdivant. "This is my three-way man here," Casey said as he introduced Elston to Ed Sullivan and thousands of TV viewers around the country. "He's the best I ever got at a lotta positions and he can do a number of things which a lot of them can't." Elston came back home that night and said, "The Old Man made me feel good the way he was bragging about me."

On April 14 in Boston, Elston's name went down in Yankee history. He got into his first game when Irv Noren was ejected over a call at home plate. According to the Black Associated Press, Elston made his Yankee debut at 4:32 p.m. "Howard's appearance at-bat signaled the fall of a dynasty that had been assailed on all sides as being anti-Negro. The fans gave Howard a well-deserved round of applause, making his debut on the heretofore lily-white Bronx Bombers." Elston played three innings that day. He singled and drove in a run in an 8–4 loss to the Red Sox. Finally, the Yankees had become the thirteenth club in the major leagues to field a black player. The only holdouts were the Philadelphia Phillies, Detroit Tigers, and Boston Red Sox.

One day later, Elston got his first start, getting four hits off Boston pitcher Ike DeLock. Even more memorable was a game against Detroit in which Elston got the game-winning hit in the ninth inning, a triple off Billy Hoeft. When Elston went to the clubhouse, he found a carpet of clean white towels leading from his locker to the showers. Along the way was a guard of honor headed by Mickey Mantle and Joe Collins. Turns out it was a Yankee tradition. Elston loved it. "When they did that," Elston later said, "I figured I was accepted just like everybody else."

Another highlight was the day Elston and Bob Cerv became the first American League players ever to hit pinch-hit home runs in the same half-inning. But his rookie season was not without problems. Elston quickly learned where he could go and where he could not. In Chicago, Baltimore, and Kansas City, he had to go off by himself. Imagine the indignity. Elston would have to wait outside, often while still in uniform, while his teammates were bused or taxied back to an all-white hotel. Back then, no one on the Yankees seemed to notice or care. It was accepted. Mused one writer in the *New York Post*: "We finally let a Negro play on our team; do we have to worry about his hotel space, too? It must be painful and confusing for a man to be told he is a first-class citizen only during those hours when he's playing baseball."

James Hicks, a writer for the *Amsterdam News*, berated Elston for accepting a position as a second-class citizen on a first-class team. I wrote Hicks a letter, and he apologized. It seemed so silly. What was Elston supposed to do? Elston never liked being called an "Uncle Tom" or "token nigger," but there was nothing he could do about it. If that was the price it took for him to be a Yankee, so be it.

On Elston's first trip into Kansas City, he stayed in a black hotel. The *New York Post* sent a cityside reporter named Ted Posten to room with

Elston, but Weiss barred him, at first, because he was not an accredited baseball writer, then because he didn't want his players rooming with nonplayers. By the time the Yankees made their next trip out west, Posten had received the proper credentials and there was a big fuss in the papers.

Stengel, for one, went to bat for Elston. Casey went up to traveling secretary Bill McCorry, the man who reportedly had said "no nigger will ever have a berth on any train I'm running," after the trip and said, "Is he on this team or not?" When the Yankees got home Casey went to George Weiss. "Howard's one of my players, ain't he? If he don't stay there, we don't stay there."

A few weeks later on the second trip to Kansas City, Casey told Elston that he was to go inside the Muehlebach Hotel and get a key just like everybody else. But he would have no roommate. It would be years before Elston was allowed to have a regular roommate on the road. Later that season, though, when the Yankees made a goodwill tour of Japan, Elston and Skowron were roommates. "To me it was no big deal," Skowron recalled. "Me and Ellie were probably the first interracial roommates in baseball history."

Another funny thing happened one day on the team bus. Elston was sitting by himself when Billy Martin came aboard. Billy, with a big cigar in his mouth, came up to Elston, looked at the empty seat next to him and said, "Move over, dago." Everyone laughed. Billy had often said that to Joe DiMaggio. Now he was saying it to Elston.

In the early days, Phil Rizzuto and Yogi Berra were two of Elston's best friends on the team. Elston used to call Rizzuto "my great white father." Elston liked Kansas City from his days with the Monarchs and later the Blues. But he was downright scared that first night he had to stay in an all-white hotel. He went to his room and double-bolted the lock and put a chair by the door. "I was frightened to death," Elston recalled in 1963. Elston called Rizzuto, and they went out to dinner. They went to a place called the Italian Gardens, where Phil knew the owner. It made that night a little easier for Elston.

"Phil Rizzuto, damn, he was great. I will never forget him," Elston told author Peter Golenbock in 1977. "I give Phil the most credit of anyone. He would call me up during the day and take me out to various places, go to movies, meet people around the league. He was the type of man I respected, and I give him a lot of credit. I got pretty lonesome at times, and Phil would sense when I hit the real blues."

Yogi took to Elston right away, and they'd go to the movies on road trips. Rizzuto took Elston out to play golf. Hank Bauer was another good friend. His locker was right next to Elston's, and Elston said Hank would give him tips on playing the outfield, when to take batting practice, what to look for in certain pitchers and, of course, how to act like a Yankee. A big, mean-looking guy with a crew cut, Hank took it personally whenever Elston was heckled. It was not unusual for Hank to come out of the dugout and confront anybody giving Elston a hard time. "He was my friend," Bauer would say. "He was one of the nicest men I ever met."

Hank Bauer still remembers the second trip to Chicago. "We were staying at the Del Prado Hotel. A bunch of us were eating breakfast at a big round table and there was an empty seat right next to me. Elston came in the room, saw the seat and hedged a bit. I motioned for him to come sit with us. When he sat down I told him, 'You play with us, you eat with us. You're one of us.'"

"You hear a lot about the Yankee spirit, and the Yankee way," Elston once said. "Believe me, it is not exaggerated."

Andy Carey was impressed with the way Elston handled himself. "He did his job under tremendous pressure," Carey said. "Elston knew what he had to do. He knew the world was watching. He did what Jackie Robinson did, and he did it for the Yankees. He worked hard, he hustled, he did everything he had to."

Elston played in 97 games in the 1955 season, 79 as an outfielder and nine as a catcher. He batted .290 with 10 home runs and 43 RBIs. Playing left field was never easy. Left field at Yankee Stadium was the worst sun field in baseball. There was no such thing as a routine fly ball. Carey called it a "high sky." Yogi Berra said it best: When someone asked how tough it was to play left field, he said, "It gets late out there early."

"I can still see Elston out there fighting the sun on his hands and knees," recalls infielder Jerry Coleman. "He may have been a catcher, but as an outfielder he got the job done."

Yogi hit .272 with 22 home runs and 108 RBIs and again was named Most Valuable Player. "The only thing holding him back," Casey said of Elston, "is that there is a man named Mr. Berra. All I know is that he's my good-luck charm. Whenever I put him in my lineup, we win pennants."

If there was one thing Elston did not like about Stengel, it was Casey's love of the platoon system. "You can substitute, but you can rarely replace," Casey said. "With Howard, I have a replacement, not a substitute." Casey had so many great players, and took great delight in using the younger ones to motivate the older players. "We all got along with Casey rotten," Coleman says. "Casey treated us all pretty much the same. Even Elston. No doubt he loved Mantle, Berra, and Martin, but other than that he was fair." Said Andy Carey, "Elston was treated like everybody else on the team. He was a star performer, but remember, everybody else was, too."

Sometimes Elston would be taken out for a pinch-hitter against a right-handed pitcher and he'd come home all upset, very moody or temperamental. This was the first time in his career he had been forced to sit on the bench. Sometimes he would come home and not talk at all. All I could say was, "Be patient." There was always the possibility of a trade. Baltimore reportedly offered one hundred thousand dollars for Elston. But Elston wanted to make it with the Yankees, not someone else. Elston and I had a few arguments about this. I used to tell him he should be like Willie Mays. I told him they were not going to play him over Yogi. Why were they making him a catcher? To me, it was just another way of holding him back. It was very frustrating, but he was determined to play for only one team.

The Yankees had so many talented players, they believed they should win every ball game. And when they didn't, it showed in the clubhouse.

There was pressure to win every day. Casey would threaten the players to motivate them, telling them things like, "If you don't do that, we'll back up the truck and trade your butt to Kansas City." One day, Elston was in the locker listening to a bunch of teammates talking about the stock market. "Fellas," barked Casey, "I got a good stock for you. Buy all the railroad stock you can get because when we start shipping you fellas back to the bush leagues next week, the railroads is going to get rich."

The Yankees won the pennant that year and played the Dodgers in the World Series. By that time I was seven months pregnant, and the doctor had told me to go back to St. Louis, where I could stay with my mother. Yvonne Crowe, George's wife, told me, "If my husband was in the World Series, I'd be there." Instead I had to watch Elston on TV with everyone else in my family.

Everyone in St. Louis already knew what a terrific athlete Elston was. And Elston became a hero when he homered in his first World Series at-bat. The Yankees were losing 3–0 in Game 1 when Joe Collins walked in the second inning. With Don Newcombe pitching, Elston knocked a fastball over the left-field fence as the Yankees rallied for a 6–5 victory at Yankee Stadium. Elston's mother and Rev. Baker were elated. It made us all so happy. Later, Elston said hitting that homer was the greatest highlight of his major-league career.

After the home run off Newcombe, Elston struggled. Hank Bauer pulled a hamstring, and Elston played some right field. He only had two other hits in the Series and struck out eight times. The Yankees won Game 2, but were swept three straight games at Ebbets Field. In Game 3, Jackie Robinson decoyed Elston, playing left field, into throwing to the wrong base. Jackie had doubled and made a wide turn coming around second. When Elston got the ball, he threw the ball to second base, and Jackie hustled into third. Elston was embarrassed.

The Yankees won Game 6, even though Elston struck out three times. He was so upset with himself after that third strikeout that he smashed his bat over the dugout roof. It was obvious that Elston was trying too hard, but Casey kept faith in him for Game 7. "He's going to play," said Casey. "He's all right. He's just pressing too hard. If only he'd stop trying to overkill the ball and hit one ball to the opposite field, then he'd be all right. The pitchers are playing him for a sucker."

The Dodgers won Game 7 behind Johnny Podres, 2–0. That was the game in which Sandy Amoros made an amazing catch in the left-field corner to rob Yogi of a hit. But it was Elston who made the game's final out when he grounded out to Pee Wee Reese at shortstop. Elston took it hard. The Yankees had always beaten the Dodgers in the World Series, and the first time he gets to play in the World Series, they lose and he makes the final out.

Elston called me in St. Louis that night. There was sadness in his voice, but he promised me that the Yankees would beat the Dodgers the following year if the Dodgers were "lucky enough" to make it back to the World Series. Elston took the loss with class. Like a Yankee.

CHAPTER SEVEN

The Bronx, 1956

Elston Howard remained with the Yankees not only because he proved himself a fine player, but because he was quiet, well-behaved, a fine asset to the off-the-field tone on the club. He was always cognizant of the fact that he was a Negro. He would receive more attention, and from bigots, possibly more criticism than if he had been a Caucasian.
—DAN DANIEL, SPORTING NEWS, FEBRUARY 1, 1956

THE LONELIEST MAN IN JAPAN IN THE FALL OF 1955 ALSO WAS THE happiest. Elston and the Yankees were on their way to the Far East just hours after losing Game 7 of the 1955 World Series to the Brooklyn Dodgers. While the Yankees were en route to becoming the first American baseball team to make a goodwill tour of Japan, I stayed at home in St. Louis awaiting the birth of our first child. Of course, I wanted to go oh so badly. I wasn't joking around when I said, "Why can't I go? I could have the baby in Japan and Elston Jr. could have dual citizenship." All the players brought their wives, except Elston and Mickey Mantle. Like me, Merlyn Mantle was pregnant, expecting their second son.

This wasn't Elston's first trip to Japan. He was stationed there in 1951 when he served in the army. This time he was there for a three-week barnstorming tour. First they were in Hawaii, then Wake Island, Guam, the Philippines, and finally Japan. Elston developed a strong interest in photography and bought a sixteen-millimeter Bolex movie camera for the trip. He and Andy Carey filmed everything in sight. Elston and Andy were always good friends. They would stay up half the night on road trips talking about photography and taking pictures. When the Japan trip ended, Andy took all of Elston's film and they turned it into a documentary that they gave to their teammates.

While he was away, Elston phoned me just about every chance he got. In fact, it was Casey Stengel's idea, and Casey himself paid for the phone calls. On November 4, 1955, the day of our first wedding anniversary, they wheeled me into the delivery room at People's Hospital. While I was in labor, I received a phone call from Elston. At Casey's insistence, it was switched to me in the delivery room. The Yankee organization was very thoughtful. After I delivered Elston Jr., my room was filled with all sorts of flowers, courtesy of the Yankees.

Elston was jubilant. He told me he wanted to come home so badly. The Yankees went 23–0–1 on the tour, and Elston was their leading hitter with a .468 average. After every game, the game's top player was awarded a kimono. Elston came home with a closet full. While he was in Japan, Elston got to talk to Casey quite a bit. One night Casey kept him up until five in the morning talking about Satchel Paige and then had him playing nine innings the very next day. "I felt like a dishrag," Elston told the *Post*'s Maury Allen.

With a new son to feed, Elston expressed concern to Casey that he would need to make more money. Casey promised he would take care of that when they got home. Yet weeks later when Elston, back in St. Louis, received his 1956 contract in the mail, it called for him to make seven thousand dollars, just a thousand more than he made his rookie season. Elston ran into Stan Musial at a local YMCA dinner and told him about the contract. Musial said to hang in there; he'd get another offer.

Not too long later, another contract arrived, calling for Elston to make ten thousand dollars. Elston signed it and sent it right back to George Weiss. Elston was so happy; we made a down payment on a new house in St. Louis. Imagine, ten thousand dollars. We thought we were rich!

Before spring training, Casey told Dan Daniel of the *World-Telegram* that Elston was one of nine Yankee players who were indispensable. The others were Mantle, Berra, Hank Bauer, Whitey Ford, Bob Turley, Gil

McDougald, Billy Martin, and Andy Carey. Casey also promised that Elston would play more and Yogi, who would soon be thirty-one years old, would play less.

"Apparently I used him too much," Casey said of Berra, who had played 140 games in earning his second straight MVP award. "But we needed Howard in the outfield, and the [pennant] race continued so rough and tough I had to have Yogi's bat every day. Well, I plan to catch Yogi twice a week.

"Now, about this here Howard. He can do three things well—catch, pinch-hit, and play right field. I used him quite a lot in left and want to say I have seen better left fielders.

"We have had quite a few inquiries about Howard. But like I told you a year ago, when so many wise guys were yammering that the Yankees did not really intend to have a Negro player, he is not to be traded."

Casey also had some words about Phil Rizzuto, one of Elston's closest friends on the team: "Rizzuto played fine ball in the World Series, but seven games are not a season. When a guy gets to be thirty-seven at a spot like short, his manager has to start making other arrangements."

In early February, with Elston Jr., we loaded up the Pontiac and left St. Louis for spring training in Florida. In those days when you drove through the South, you had to map out your overnight stays in advance. There were no Holiday Inns for black people. Rev. Baker, Elston's godfather, came up with a suggestion. He told us about a dear friend of his, a minister from Georgia who had a son in Montgomery, Alabama. He, too, was a minister. Perhaps we could stay the night with him. "You'll like him," Rev. Baker told Elston. "He's a nice man, a progressive thinker." His name was Martin Luther King.

We were on our way to Florida, just outside of Montgomery, when Elston called Dr. King on the phone to ask for directions. But when Elston came back to the car, he seemed shaken. "We can't stay there," Elston told me. "His house has just been fire-bombed. The police are there now." We continued down the road and found a room that night at a flophouse. It was awful. There were bed bugs and it was not very clean. But the owner recognized Elston and he did invite us to dinner at his house right across the street.

It was always an adventure driving through the South, but we had problems in the North, too. One time we were driving from New York back to St. Louis. When we got into Ohio, Elston was turned down every time we stopped at a motel and he asked for a room. After about the fifth or sixth time, he got so frustrated that he suggested that I try to get a room. At the next motel we stopped at, I went in and got the room without any trouble. It didn't matter that Elston played for the New York Yankees. As far as motel clerks were concerned, he was just another black man.

When we arrived in St. Petersburg in 1956, Elston once again was not allowed to stay in the Soreno Hotel. The only place we could go was back to Mr. Williams's boardinghouse.

When Elston reported to camp the next day, he was greeted by teammate Tom Sturdivant.

"You got the family with you, I hear," Sturdivant said. "Great. It's good for a fellow."

Said Elston, "Kid woke me up too early this morning. He sleeps in the day. I got to get him to sleep in the night."

"Still just one kid?" Sturdivant joked. "What's the matter with you, Ellie?"

Elston laughed. "More than one," he said, "and I wouldn't get any sleep at all."

Casey may not have been too happy about Elston's play in left field, but he had little choice but to play him there. Irv Noren was back, but he was recovering from surgery on both knees. There was Norm Siebern, a left-handed-hitting rookie outfielder. Like Elston, Bob Turley, and Yogi, Siebern grew up in the St. Louis area. Elston had never played against him, but he had read about him in the newspapers.

When spring training began, Casey reiterated his plans for Elston. "I hope to give Yogi twenty-five games off and use Howard more, not only as a starting catcher, but to finish games we might be losing," he said.

On March 17 Elston fractured the fourth finger on his right hand on a foul tip by Detroit's Charley King. Sidney Gaynor, the team doctor, said Elston would miss at least three weeks. Five days later, Siebern crashed into the left-field wall and injured his left knee. So much for Casey's plans. When the season opened on April 17, Elston was back. Batting seventh, he played left field and went 1-for-5. In fact, that season Elston only caught in twenty-eight games. In sixty-five games he played the outfield or was a pinch-hitter.

In 1956, Mickey Mantle had a tremendous season, winning the Triple Crown. Elston loved Mickey, but he thought it was somewhat funny how much Mickey would go out and party. Elston would sometimes come home laughing and shaking his head. He'd tell me about the games when he and Mickey would run out to the outfield together before a game and Mickey would say, "Hey, Elston, I had a rough night. Anything close, you get it."

One of the highlights that year was my appearance on the *Ed Sullivan Show*, along with several other Yankee wives. Gil McDougald's nephew had some rare disease, and the wives formed a group called the Yankee Pinch Hitters. We did fashion shows and raised money for certain charities. On the night of August 12, I was the star of the show. When we got on stage, Ed introduced me as "Mrs. Elston Howard." I was so excited, I just kept on talking about our group and how good the Yankees were, and Ed couldn't get me to stop.

The Yankees got off to a good start that season, but the Chicago White Sox provided some stiff competition. They swept a four-game set from the Yankees in late June, leaving them just two games back before the All-Star break. But with Mickey Mantle in the middle of his Triple Crown season, the Yankees began to pull away. By late August the team was comfortably in front of the White Sox and on their way to another pennant. On August 22, Elston was hitting .252 with five home runs and 21 RBIs.

Three days later, Phil Rizzuto was released on Old-Timer's Day. Elston felt so bad for him. When he needed a friend in the Yankee clubhouse, Phil was always there. He and his wife, Cora, would quite often invite us out to dinner. When Elston was on the road, they would go to the movies.

To make matters worse, when the Yankees cut Rizzuto, they got Enos "Country" Slaughter from Kansas City. Slaughter was a forty-year-old left-handed hitter who played left field. A future Hall of Famer,

Slaughter played for the St. Louis Cardinals in the '40s. In 1947 he allegedly tried to organize a player strike when Jackie Robinson played his first game in St. Louis. Slaughter never was accepted by his Yankee teammates, but Casey appreciated his hustle and confrontational attitude. One time he supposedly spit on Moose Skowron's shoes for no reason at all. On the Yankees, Slaughter was a loner who was always running—to his position in left field or even to first base. Some of the Yankees thought he was a bald-headed showboat. Several of the Yankee wives told me that he supposedly had pushed his wife out of a moving car.

With Slaughter around, Elston didn't play much the final month of the season. By then the Yankees were in first by ten games, and the only question was who would be their opponent in the World Series. Brooklyn was in a big pennant race with Cincinnati and Milwaukee. We were pulling for the Reds because George Crowe had been traded to their team. George was known as "Big Daddy" by the press because the young black players, Elston included, often would come to him for advice. In the late '40s he played pro basketball with Jackie Robinson and Irv Noren on a team called the Los Angeles Red Devils. When the team broke up a few months later, Robinson went on to the Brooklyn Dodgers and George signed up with the New York Black Yankees. In 1949 he signed with the Boston Braves and in later years barnstormed with Elston on the Roy Campanella All-Stars.

In 1956 the Reds finished two games behind the Dodgers. Years later, George Crowe told us that his manager, Birdie Tebbetts, was the reason why. "He didn't want to win the pennant," George said. "We had a pitcher named Brooks Lawrence who won thirteen straight games. But Birdie Tebbetts came out one day and told someone, 'Ain't no black man's going to win twenty games for me.' And he refused to pitch Lawrence after he got nineteen wins." Good God Almighty! Can you believe that?

There also was the time George said his own teammate asked an opposing pitcher to throw at him. "Joe Adcock didn't like me," George recalls. "So one day he goes over to Art Fowler before the game and tells him 'to knock that big nigger down.' Art couldn't understand that at all."

As for Elston, he had a so-so season. One game in late June he was taken to the hospital in Cleveland after he broke out in welts. The doctors said they were the result of nerves. They said he was worrying too much. He finished the '56 season with five homers, 34 RBIs, and a .259 average. He was very moody that year. He knew he could do better. How could he prove that he was better than anybody else when Casey's platoon system was keeping him down? Of course, Elston should have been playing every day, and I told him so. For Elston, however, asking for a trade was out of the question. Things didn't get better in the World Series, either. Just before the start, Elston was hospitalized for a few days with strep throat. It was too bad because Elston's father, Travis, came to New York to watch him play. Elston's relationship with his father was still strained, but at least they were trying to get along. I was sitting next to Travis on October 8 when Don Larsen pitched his perfect game, and Yogi was the catcher. Elston couldn't believe it. "I would have given everything I owned to catch that game," he told me that night.

The Yankees lost Game 6 in Brooklyn when Slaughter misplayed a ball hit by Jackie Robinson in the tenth inning. Afterward, Billy Martin, according to one newspaper report, supposedly went to Casey and told him, "If you're going to keep playing that National League bobo out there, we're going to blow this World Series. You better put Elston out there and you better get Skowron back on first base."

In Game 7 at Ebbets Field, Casey did just that. Elston and Moose, both right-handed hitters, started against right-hander Don Newcombe. Yogi homered in his first two at-bats as the Yankees took a 4–0 lead. In the fourth inning with the bases empty, Elston belted a Newcombe fastball high to the opposite field, over the scoreboard in right-center. It was Elston's second World Series homer, both coming at Newcombe's expense.

The Yankees increased their lead to 9–0 in the seventh when Moose Skowron hit a grand slam. For good measure, Elston followed with a double off the wall. That was it. The Yankees were champions again.

That night the Yankees threw a big party that lasted all night at the Waldorf Astoria's Starlight Roof. One of the highlights was when Casey's wife, Edna, asked Elston to dance. Everybody got a kick out of that.

Sadly, Jackie Robinson went hitless in Game 7, and it turned out to be his final major-league baseball game. Shortly after the World Series, the Dodgers traded him to the New York Giants. The Giants were look-ing for a first baseman. Their red-hot rookie, a hard-hitting youngster from Ohio named Bill White, had been drafted into the army. But Jackie decided he would rather quit than play for the Giants.

One year later, the Dodgers were on their way to Los Angeles and the Giants to San Francisco. New York was left with only one major-league baseball team and only one black major-league player.

Elston Howard as a thirteen-year-old in St. Louis.

Me (second from left) with (from left) sisters Martha and Loyette, brother Eddie, and Aunt Louise.

Teannie Edwards, former Negro Leagues player,
manager of the black St. Louis Braves, and the
man who discovered Elston Howard.
COURTESY OF FRANK EDWARDS.

Elston (left) with some of his army buddies.

Elston tries on a Yankee uniform for the first time at his mother's house in
St. Louis in 1954.

Elston with Bill Williams in St. Petersburg, Florida, for spring training in 1955. The Yankees and other teams relied on Williams to find housing for black players in the spring, because St. Petersburg hotels refused to take them.

Elston in 1955, his rookie season, in which he became the first black to play for the New York Yankees.

Elston and me at a fruit market in 1955. His eating habits were instilled in him by his mother, a dietitian, and throughout his baseball career he sought out fresh fruit in the cities he traveled to.

Elston makes a running catch in front of Mickey Mantle during a game in September 1955. Although his natural position was at catcher, early in his career he spent much of his time platooning in the outfield and even at first base.
COURTESY OF THE *NEW YORK TIMES.*

Me, Elston, and Elston Jr. in 1956.

Me and Elston at home with our record collection.

In the 1950s black major-leaguers from different teams formed close bonds, especially while playing together overseas on winter-league teams and sharing often substandard accommodations during spring training. In this photo, Joe Black of the Brooklyn Dodgers, Willie Mays of the New York Giants, Elston, and the Giants' Monte Irvin team up for a YMCA charity basketball game.

Elston with his first Yankee manager, Casey Stengel. He admired Stengel, despite Casey's occasional racial remarks, which Elston discounted as the product of an older generation. But he chafed under Stengel's system of platooning several players at the same position.

Elston and Yogi Berra. Although they competed at the same position, they established a warm friendship—as I did with Yogi's wife, Carmen—and each held the other in great esteem as a teammate.

COURTESY OF THE NEW YORK YANKEES BASEBALL CLUB.

The imposing Yankee lineup of the late 1950s and early 1960s included Mickey Mantle, Yogi Berra, Bill Skowron, Gil McDougald, Elston, and Roger Maris.
COURTESY OF THE NEW YORK YANKEES BASEBALL CLUB.

Elston with teammates Tony Kubek (left) and Mickey Mantle at the start of the 1960 World Series against the Pittsburgh Pirates.

Elston's hand is examined by, from left, trainer Gus Mauch, manager Casey Stengel, and coach Ralph Houk after being hit by a pitch in the second inning of Game Six of the 1960 World Series. The injury would force Elston to sit out the rest of the Series, including the dramatic Game Seven loss in which the Pirates' Bill Mazeroski homered in the bottom of the ninth to win the championship for Pittsburgh.

Elston is greeted at home plate by teammates Bill Skowron, Bobby Richardson, and Yogi Berra after homering against Detroit during the 1961 season.
COURTESY OF THE *NEW YORK TIMES*.

Bill Skowron, Whitey Ford, and Elston, after winning Game One of the 1961 World Series against the Cincinnati Reds. Skowron had come up through the minor leagues with Elston; Ford's nickname, "Chairman of the Board," was bestowed on him by his batterymate.

Elston demonstrates his strong arm in a game against the Chicago White Sox during the 1962 season.

Elston slides in ahead of Cincinnati shortstop Eddie Kasko's tag for a double during Game Three of the 1961 World Series.
COURTESY OF THE ASSOCIATED PRESS.

The Yankees on the set of a Broadway show. From left: Bill Skowron, actor Jim Backus, Yogi Berra, Jack Kelly, Whitey Ford, Bob Cerv, Elston, and Hector Lopez.

The Howard family in 1962: Cheryl, Karen, Elston Jr., Elston, and me.

Elston and Elston Jr., probably reading the sports page together.

The Howards at our new house in Teaneck, New Jersey, in 1963.

Elston and me in our new home, with some of our art collection.

Me and Elston with our good friends Fran and Bernie Miller in 1963. Bernie, publisher of *Gentleman's Quarterly* magazine, met Elston soon after he began playing for the Yankees.

Elston Howard Night at Yankee Stadium, August 29, 1964. Elston's mother, Emmaline, is next to me, with Cheryl and Elston Jr. The piano was one of many gifts Elston received.

COURTESY OF BOB OLEN, *NEW YORK POST*.

Me with Elston in May of 1965, after Elston's elbow surgery. In the '65 season age and injuries caught up to the Yankees. The team would not win another American League pennant for more than a decade.

PHOTO BY WILLIAM JACOBELLIS.

COURTESY OF THE *NEW YORK POST*.

On August 3, 1967, Elston was traded to the Boston Red Sox. It was a sad day for him, but he arrived in Boston just in time to help them win the "Impossible Dream" pennant. He finished his playing career with the Red Sox, retiring after the 1968 season.
Courtesy of Fred Keenan, *Patriot Ledger*, Quincy, Massachusetts.

Elston's retirement didn't last long—by the beginning of the 1969 season he was back with the Yankees, this time as a coach. This photo was taken during spring training in 1972.
COURTESY OF THE NEW YORK YANKEES BASEBALL CLUB.

One of Elston's coaching duties during the "Bronx Zoo" years of the 1970s was to play peacemaker to volatile personalities such as manager Billy Martin. "Elston was a pretty good bouncer," said first baseman Chris Chambliss; pitcher Ron Guidry called him a "calming presence."

Elston at home in May of 1979, with his Gold Glove and American League MVP trophies. By the 1979 season, his health prevented him from taking the field as a Yankee coach.

PHOTO BY RICHARD LEE. COURTESY OF THE *NEW YORK POST*.

Elston and Roger Maris are immortalized, their plaques added to "Monument Valley" in Yankee Stadium, in 1984. Elston Jr. and I stand behind Elston's plaque, while Roger addresses the crowd.

COURTESY OF BOB OLEN, *NEW YORK POST*.

Cheryl Howard sings the national anthem at Yankee Stadium, one of several occasions on which she has been invited to perform the song before a Yankee game.

CHAPTER EIGHT

Casey's Machine

*Elston's fine showing in the Series emphasizes the fact that of all the
Yankees, he is the most underrated.*
—FRANK GRAHAM, *NEW YORK JOURNAL-AMERICAN*, 1958

BARNSTORMING. THIRTY DAYS TO MAKE EXTRA MONEY. ELSTON LOVED
doing it, and believe me, we needed the money. He was with Roy Campanella's All-Stars after the 1956 season. Back in those days, all the top
players went barnstorming after the season. It's hard to imagine nowadays, but just about every major-league player at that time needed a part-
time job during the off-season.

A lot of the big stars played on Campanella's team. There was Henry
Aaron, Willie Mays, Don Newcombe, George Crowe, Brooks Lawrence, Hank Thompson, and Joe Black. Many of the same players had
barnstormed for Jackie Robinson's team, but many of them quit when
they found out Jackie was making more money than anyone else. On
Campanella's team all players were equal, and they were paid accordingly.
Elston also occasionally would play for the Mickey Mantle All-Stars,
often against the Willie Mays All-Stars. Everybody had fun. One weekend, I left Elston Jr. behind with his grandmother Emmaline in St. Louis
and joined Elston for a weekend in New Orleans. It was the first time
I had gone to New Orleans and, of course, the first time I had gumbo.
When I was there the players joked about the way Joe Black would eat,

eat, and eat, how he'd sit in the back of the bus with a dozen doughnuts and a six-pack of Coca-Cola.

The barnstorming tours usually went throughout the South and, sometimes, to the Caribbean. Elston loved the camaraderie, the games, and the fact that he was earning the extra money, about one hundred dollars a game, depending on the gate. It was about this time that Elston and Don Newcombe became very good friends. In later years, Don opened a nightclub in Newark, and Elston would always bring his friends or business partners there to be entertained. Elston and Campanella got along pretty well, though we rarely socialized with players from the Brooklyn Dodgers or New York Giants. I do remember going to a big backyard barbecue at Monte Irvin's house in Montclair, New Jersey. It was a fundraiser, I think, for the NAACP, and of course Willie Mays was there. We had gotten to know Willie pretty well from our days in Puerto Rico, and then we lived across the street on Edgecombe Avenue. Willie had this big Cadillac. One day he gave my sister Loyette a ride to the airport. Willie had girlfriends all over the place. On one trip to Puerto Rico, he bought a dozen Christmas gifts for his girlfriends. Each gift was the same thing.

Once the major-league baseball season ended, Elston would barnstorm and I would head back to St. Louis. We still considered it home. We owned a house there; our families were still there. With Elston Jr. now about a year old, we needed a larger place. We eventually moved into an apartment on the Grand Concourse in the Bronx. It was in a totally lily-white area. We only got that apartment because someone from the Yankee front office got it for us.

Soon after, Elston and I decided we were going to need a home in the New York area. Elston called up Jackie Robinson for financial advice. Jackie was connected to a bank in Harlem, the Carver Savings Bank, and helped us get the money we would later need to buy our first house in New Jersey.

Even with the World Series check, we were still struggling to make ends meet. For the '57 season, Elston was only going to make fourteen thousand dollars, compared to Yogi at fifty-eight thousand and Mickey Mantle at sixty thousand. George Weiss was the general manager. The man was a dog when it came to negotiating contracts. Boy, could we have used an agent, but they did not exist back then. Weiss would always point to those World Series checks as if they were taken for granted as part of your income.

Elston was able to supplement his income with a few commercial endorsements, thanks mostly to Frank Scott, the man who helped many of the Yankee players line up commercial spots. Even though Elston wasn't much of a drinker and didn't smoke at all, we had a deal with Ballantine Beer and another with Kool Cigarettes. Ballantine was one of the Yankees' big radio sponsors, and they named him to the sales staff. Ballantine paid Elston to give clinics or speak at dinners; he received about one hundred dollars for each appearance.

Still, Elston's endorsements were geared for black customers. Only in Harlem could you see billboards of Elston and Ballantine Beer. Meanwhile, other Yankee stars were getting big money; Yogi made good money from Yoo-Hoo soft-drink commercials. Elston always talked about how blacks could not get the same commercials. Gillette signed a bunch of white players to do commercials, but no blacks. As Elston would say, "We gotta shave, too." The Louisville Slugger bat company was another problem. The company was selling Elston's bats, but he always had trouble getting money for it. It was always a fight.

In spring camp in 1957 in St. Petersburg, optimism was quite high. There was a good batch of promising rookies, notably Marv Throneberry, Bobby Richardson, Woodie Held, and Tony Kubek. Kubek was twenty years old, but he was the best of the bunch. He could play center field, shortstop, and platoon with Elston in left field. Said Casey, "Kubek gets on base a lot, goes from first to third, can take care of himself, is a fine, quiet, well-behaved, well-conditioned young man. He obeys the rules, gets lots of sleep, drinks plenty of orange juice, does not overeat, writes to his father, and what with one thing and another, is OK!"

With Kubek around, Casey was once again promising that Elston would get more work behind the plate. That was the case until early March when Moose Skowron broke his thumb and Casey decided to try Elston out at first base. Elston was never comfortable at first base, but he played eighty-five games there in his career, and it kept him in the lineup and off Casey's bench.

On opening day in Boston, Elston started in left field and went 1-for-4, driving in the deciding run with a ninth-inning single. But the Yanks got off to a slow start that season. By May 24 they were in third place with a 17–12 record. Leading the league were the Cleveland Indians, whom the Yankees saw as their biggest threat. The Indians had a good pitching staff that included left-hander Herb Score, who struck out a lot of batters with a wicked fastball. He had been named Rookie of the Year in 1955; Elston finished second in the voting.

In early May the Yankees went to Cleveland for a big showdown. It was a series that Elston would never forget. On May 7, Elston saw his good friend Gil McDougald line a hard shot that hit Score in the face, practically crushing his eye socket. It was a terrible thing to see. McDougald was quite shaken. "If anything happens to his eye, I will quit baseball," he said. Herb Score made it back, although he was never the same player. But neither was McDougald, who eventually retired in 1960 rather than be traded away. The Yankees beat the Indians in that series and soon embarked on a nine-game winning streak. Back in New York, about a week later, there was another incident Elston would never forget.

May 15 was Billy Martin's twenty-ninth birthday, and the Yankees had no game that day. Mickey Mantle organized a dinner party at a restaurant called Danny's Hideaway. Yogi, Hank Bauer, and Whitey Ford brought their wives. Elston and I were invited to go, but we couldn't find a baby-sitter, and it was a good thing, too. After dinner, everyone decided to head over to the Copacabana Club to see Sammy Davis Jr. As the story goes, a bunch of drunk bowlers at the next table began heckling Davis, calling him a bunch of racist names. After Hank Bauer told them to shut up, they started giving the Yankees a hard time, too. Minutes later, one of the bowlers was beaten up in the bathroom. The man claimed Hank did it, but Hank denied it. The man, a deli owner from Queens named Edwin Jones, probably was beaten up by one of the bouncers. Hank saw the man lying on the floor bleeding; the players grabbed their wives and made a quick getaway through the kitchen. But the next day the story was all over the newspapers. When George Weiss found out, Yogi, Billy, Mickey, and Hank were fined one thousand dollars each, despite their innocence. I told Elston, "We did our own baby-sitting and saved a thousand dollars."

That incident was about the last straw for Billy Martin. He and Mickey were the best of friends, but Yankee management knew what they were up to. As soon as Bobby Richardson proved that he could handle second base and hit major-league pitching, we knew Billy was a goner. The end came a few weeks later, just before the trading deadline. The Yankees were playing Chicago, and Art Ditmar and Minnie Minoso came to blows over a beanball incident. Larry Doby was then playing for the White Sox and he got involved, as did Billy. The next inning Billy asked Ditmar what Doby had said to him. "He said he was gonna stick a knife in me," Ditmar said. Billy went off. He ran up to Doby and began punching him. Two days later, he was traded to Kansas City.

Elston, of course, was sad to see Billy go. Billy was a tough, gutty player, one of Casey's favorites, and Elston always appreciated his friendship, his we-against-them attitude, and his hustling style of play. But he also was a party boy. If anything good came from that trade, it was that the number of black players on the Yankee roster doubled. In exchange for Martin, the Yankees got Ryne Duren and also Harry Simpson, a left-handed, pull-hitting outfielder. Finally, Elston had himself a roommate. Harry Simpson was called "Suitcase" because he played for seventeen teams in eleven years. Casey at one point called him the best defensive outfielder in the American League. In 1956, he had hit .293 with 21 home runs and 105 RBIs for Kansas City and was chosen by Casey for the American League All-Star team. He was hitting nearly .300 when he came to the Yankees, but he slumped badly. Harry Simpson, thirty-one years old in 1957, never made much of an impact with the Yankees, and we never got to know him. He was traded back to Kansas City during the 1958 season and retired one year later. Sad to say, Harry died in 1979.

After the Martin trade, the Yankees ran off another nine-game winning streak and were on their way to another pennant. They finished 96–55, seven games ahead of the White Sox, and were in first place for 108 days. Elston finished the season batting .253, with eight homers and 44 RBIs in 110 games.

One of the highlights of the season was when Casey named Elston to his first American League All-Star team. Even though he didn't get to play in the game, Elston was happy to be there, particularly since the game was in St. Louis. When it came time to play the '57 World Series, the Yankees had a new opponent. The Milwaukee Braves had a strong team led by Henry Aaron and Eddie Mathews, with a good pitching staff anchored by Warren Spahn and Lew Burdette. In Game 1 at Yankee Stadium, Whitey Ford and Elston helped the Yankees to a 3–1 win. Elston came off the bench to replace Moose Skowron at first base in the sixth inning. In the eighth inning of a 1–1 game, Elston singled to right field, Berra walked, and Elston scored the go-ahead run on Andy Carey's RBI single. In Game 2, the Yankees lost 4–2 to Burdette, who allegedly threw a spitball. Elston replaced Yogi late in the game and got an infield single behind second base in the ninth to start a rally. But after Kubek singled, Hank Bauer grounded into a double play.

The Yankees went to Milwaukee for Game 3 and were 12–3 winners as Kubek hit two home runs. Elston pinch-hit for Harry Simpson and walked. He replaced Skowron at first, but was 0-for-2 in his other at-bats. Although the Yankees lost the fourth game, it was one of Elston's most memorable. It was October 6. Warren Spahn started for Milwaukee. Elston started at first base, but was hitless when he came to bat with the Yankees trailing 4–1 with two out in the ninth. Milwaukee manager Fred Haney came out to the mound and told Spahn to pitch Elston outside. Then, on a 3–2 pitch, Elston blasted a curve over the wire fence in left field for a three-run homer. Suddenly, the game was tied. Asked by a reporter what Haney had said to him on the mound, Spahn said, "He told me not to do what I then did."

The Yankees took a 5–4 lead in the tenth inning on Bauer's RBI triple. Casey took Elston out and replaced him with Joe Collins at first base for defensive purposes. But then came the shoe polish incident. Vernal "Nippy" Jones, pinch-hitting for Spahn, claimed to have been hit on the foot by a Tommy Byrne pitch. When he showed umpire Augie Donatelli that the ball had shoe polish on it, he was awarded first base.

Johnny Logan then doubled to tie the score, and Mathews won it with a two-run homer.

The Yankees also lost the fifth game when Burdette outdueled Ford. Whitey pitched his heart out, but was on the wrong end of a 1–0 decision. Elston pinch-hit for Whitey in the eighth inning and was called out looking on a pitch that was low and outside. Elston sat on the bench in Game 6, won by Bob Turley and the Yankees 3–2. But he did see some action in Game 7. Elston was a late-inning replacement for Yogi and went hitless in one at-bat. The Yankees lost, and Elston finished his third World Series with three hits in eleven at-bats.

After the Series, each of the Yankees received a full share of $5,606.06. Each of the Braves got $8,924.36. Some of the Braves ridiculed the Yankees. Spahn and Burdette were quoted in the papers as saying that the Yankees would be a "second-division team" in the National League.

After the '57 season, Stengel again expressed concern about his team, notably Yogi. "Now about Berra; he is thirty-two. This past season he dropped to .251. True, he hit 24 home runs and drove in 82 runs, but he wasn't the old Yogi. It is possible that from now on he will need more help than I have been giving him. We will be ready to do that in 1958 with Elston Howard possibly confining himself to catching and Johnny Blanchard coming up from Denver.

"It would be a great thing if I could fix the situation in left field and give Howard more work behind the bat. Now don't misunderstand me, I ain't retiring Yogi not just yet, not for some years."

Casey also said the Yankees needed some outfield help. He wasn't happy with the defensive exploits of Slaughter, Simpson, or Elston. Mantle, the 1957 MVP, had leg problems. Skowron was having back problems. Joe Collins had retired. To make matters worse, Kubek was drafted into the army.

By the start of the 1958 season, I had become pregnant. At that point we were still living in an apartment at the Grand Concourse Plaza, and again we needed more space. Elston had signed a contract for $16,250. We sold the house in St. Louis and began looking for one in New Jersey. George Crowe and Whitey Ford were living on Long Island, but Elston insisted on living in New Jersey, where there was no income tax at that time. Phil Rizzuto lived there, as did Yogi, Gil McDougald, Bill Skowron, and Johnny Kucks. Elston asked Yogi and several other Yankees if they had any ideas, but even Yogi had no idea where black people lived. Of course, no one suggested that we look in their neighborhoods. We looked in Tenafly, where Gil McDougald and Yogi lived around the corner from each other. That's where I would have liked to have gone at the time, but there were no blacks in that area. So we settled on Teaneck. Elston liked Teaneck. It was close to the George Washington Bridge, just about a ten-minute drive from Yankee Stadium. We looked at about twenty houses until we found a beautiful little split-level house on Howland Avenue, in the northwest part of town. The neighborhood was integrated; there were two other black families on our street. Two doors down was Al Hibbler, the singer in Duke Ellington's band.

Our daughter, Cheryl, was born on May 9. On opening day in Boston, Elston started behind the plate and caught Don Larsen. Elston had an excellent year at the plate and was named to the American League All-Star team for the second straight season. By August 5 he was hitting .342, and suddenly it was thought he could win a batting title. He also had the best RBI average per plate appearance. But in reality, Elston was still a part-time player. He needed 477 plate appearances to qualify for the batting title. To get that many, he had to move up to one of the top three spots in the lineup, but Casey would not hear of it. "There's nothing I'd like to see better, of course, than for him to win it," Casey said. "Well, I'm not gonna catch him every day and not have him ready for what I want when I need him. I'm still thinking about winning ball games and I'm not gonna worry about twistin' everything around for one man. I'm not worryin' about that and neither is he."

But Elston was worrying about it. It was a very frustrating time because he should have been a regular player. He was in his prime, and 1958 should have been one of his best years. I told him, "If you don't play, they won't pay you." Ted Williams won the battling title with a .328 average. Elston finished at .314, but he only had 398 at-bats. He played sixty-seven games behind the plate, twenty-four in the outfield, and five at first base.

The Yankees built up a seventeen-game lead and easily made it back to the 1958 World Series for a rematch with the Braves. The Series opened in Milwaukee, and Casey was optimistic. "Howard, now's he's had a very good year, and I'd like to get him in there. But Siebern, he had to go hit .300 and against what did he hit two home runs? Right, a left-hander. And Berra, he's caught Ford so many times I have to have him in there."

In Game 1, Elston started in left field and hurt his knee in the first inning when he ran into the wire fence chasing a home run by Lew Burdette. "I cut it in three places, but they say I should be able to play," Elston said after the Yankee loss. The Yankees lost Game 2 as well, and just like in 1956, they came home to Yankee Stadium with an 0–2 deficit.

In New York, ticket scalpers were getting $200 for a three-game strip of tickets worth $31.50. The Yankees won Game 3, but Casey played Norm Siebern in left field in Game 4 and he misplayed two balls. The Yankees lost, 3–0. Now the Yankees were down three games to one. Only one team, the 1925 Pittsburgh Pirates, had ever come back from a three-to-one deficit.

Then came October 6, the date on which Elston turned the World Series around. Casey started him in left field for Game 5, although Elston had never found much success hitting off Lew Burdette and had just had dental work, on a cavity, that very morning. In the top of the sixth, the Yankees were leading 1–0 with Bob Turley on the mound. After Billy Bruton singled, Red Schoendienst sliced a low line drive into short left-center field. If the ball got past Elston, Bruton would score standing up, and Schoendienst would make it to second or third. Fighting the sun, Elston charged as hard as he could. At the last second he dove full-length, extended his glove hand, and caught the ball. Bruton was around second base. Elston jumped to his feet and threw to first base to complete the double play. "I never lost a ball in the sun in my life," Elston said afterward. "I knew I had to get the ball. I skinned my knee and stomach doing it. I'm no outfielder. I'm a catcher, but the manager put me out there and I had to do the best I could. I was charging all the way. I kept telling myself I just had to get that ball."

Said Red Barber, "Had Howard missed his gamble, it would have had the Braves in front and on their way." *The World Series Record Book,* published by the *Sporting News*, said "it was the catch that was the turning point of the entire Series." A giant photo of the catch is still on display in the Great Moments Room at Yankee Stadium.

Turley went on to shut out the Braves. "Howard's catch and throw broke the Braves' back," Casey Stengel said.

The Yankees had to win Game 6, and they did. Elston had two hits and scored in a 4–3, ten-inning win. Game 7 was a classic. The score was 2–2 in the eighth inning when Elston drove in the go-ahead run with a single. Moose Skowron added a three-run homer, and the Yankees were on their way to another World Series championship.

Newspaper writers around the country praised Elston as an unsung hero. "On any other team in the majors Howard would be the No. 1 catcher," wrote Lyall Smith of the *Detroit Free Press*. "On the Yankees he is a substitute outfielder and not a great one. He says so himself. Adequate, but nothing more. Yet he made the one great play that saved the Series."

"He is a quiet man, in speech and action," wrote Frank Graham in the *New York Journal-American*. "It is, you might say, the story of his life that he started the drive that won the sixth game and drove in the run that won the seventh yet missed the headlines."

As was their custom, the Yankees had a victory celebration at the Waldorf. At one point, the band played "Dixie" and it felt like everyone in the room was looking at us, to see how we would react. Norm Siebern's wife made some crude remark about how Elston had replaced her husband in the outfield and I had to tell her off. Up to that point, I was seething inside about all the injustice going on around us. Until then, I always kept it to myself, but this time I went off.

Hank Bauer, with four home runs and a .373 batting average, was named by *Sport* magazine as the most valuable player of the World Series. The New York Baseball Writers thought otherwise. They gave Elston the Babe Ruth Award for being the "most outstanding player" in the World Series even though he had batted only .222. Hank ended up with a new sports car. Elston's big prize was a wooden plaque.

CHAPTER NINE

A New Ball Game

Yogi will make it to the Hall of Fame soon and we suspect Howard will, too. Yogi and Elston would have looked good in Cardinal uniforms.
—ROBERT L. BURNES, *ST. LOUIS GLOBE-DEMOCRAT*

IT'S A GOOD THING ELSTON LIKED AND RESPECTED YOGI BERRA SO much. There was never any professional jealousy. Yogi and Elston always got along well, and it wasn't because they both had grown up in St. Louis. Yogi grew up on the Hill, the Italian working-class neighborhood in St. Louis, about three miles away from Compton Hill. Stan Musial owned a restaurant there. In the '40s and '50s, St. Louis was very segregated. Black people never went to Dago Hill, as it was called, because those were the times. The whole country was like that.

Yogi always was such a nice guy; Elston never complained about playing in the outfield all those years and Yogi respected him for being a team player. Back then, I told Elston that if he were on any other team, someplace where he could play every day, he would be a star. But Elston would just laugh. Leaving the Yankees, a team that had won four straight pennants, was totally out of the question.

By the end of the 1958 season, the Yankees had the two best catchers in baseball. Elston always appreciated the way Yogi and Bill Dickey had worked with him to develop his catching skills. Elston said being a Yankee catcher was like being in a special fraternity. In later years, he helped tutor Thurman Munson. On and off the field, Yogi was a valuable friend.

On road trips Yogi loved talking baseball with Elston. One time, I think it was in Milwaukee, Yogi took Elston to his aunt's home and they had a big Italian dinner. Elston just loved that. When we settled down in our new home in Teaneck, Elston would hang out at the bowling alley that Yogi and Phil Rizzuto owned in nearby Clifton. Because Elston was such a team player, Yogi never felt threatened that Elston would eventually take his job. They were teammates. When we bought our house in New Jersey, it was Yogi who took a big interest. He and Carmen became very good friends of ours, and as the years went by, our families became close. Carmen and I would take turns picking up Yogi and Elston at the airport after road trips. Let me say this: Of all the Yankee wives, Carmen was the best dressed. I tried to keep up with her. We had a mutual admiration society.

Like Yogi before him, Elston was, after the 1958 postseason, a Yankee World Series hero. In his first four years with the Yankees he had collected four World Series rings, and he gave one to each of us in our immediate family. His batting average of .314 during the '58 season was the best on the club and fourth best in the American League. Everyone knew Elston was Yogi's heir apparent.

Elston knew all about the science of catching. He was quite good at "stealing" a strike for his pitcher just by positioning his glove. "Elston was a pitcher's best friend," says Bobby Shantz. "He got more strikes for his pitcher than any other catcher I saw. When the ball hit his glove, it didn't move. His glove stayed right there. Most catchers give a little. The umpires can tell the difference between great ones and not-so greats. They gave him the call."

Years later, Whitey Ford would hedge when he was asked to pick his favorite catcher. "They were both great catchers with different styles. What I really like about Elston was that he set up close to the plate. You would throw the ball to him and hear a big crack when he caught it. I would tell Yogi 'get closer like Elston,' but Yogi was afraid of getting hit. I would get so mad at Yogi. Elston had a better arm but Yogi was pretty quick getting out from behind the plate. Both called great games; I hardly ever shook them off. Both were different types of hitters."

In 1959, Yogi was thirty-four, four years older than Elston. He had hit .266 with 22 home runs in 1958. It was the first time he did not catch a hundred games. Elston played in 103 games, 67 behind the plate, hit 11 homers, and had 66 RBIs. But his 376 at-bats were just 20 more than he had collected in 1957. Herb Score, one of the best pitchers in the American league, personally rated Elston as the toughest out in the American League.

"I gotta find a place in the lineup for that fella," Casey Stengel said after the Series. "It's only justice. He earned it. He's a good hitter and he has wonderful spirit. He's gotta lotta talent."

"The Yankees are a great organization to work for and I hope I'm with them for a long time," Elston told the *Sporting News* shortly after the World Series. The *Sporting News* was Elston's Bible. He read it every week. "I'm a catcher just filling in in the outfield," he said. "I like catching much better. And that's what I hope I'll be doing most for most of the time next season. Casey will probably play Yogi a lot in right field and first base. That means I'll do a lot of work behind the plate."

Elston was given a raise to $22,500 (from $16,250) for the 1959 season. That sum did not include the $8,759.10 winner's share each Yankee got for the World Series victory over Milwaukee. After the Series, Elston and I went on a goodwill trip to Venezuela with several other major leaguers. Richie Ashburn, who played for the Phillies, came along, as did Max Pafkin, the clown prince of baseball, and a group of other major-league players. One night there was a big dinner and they served a native dish called hiyakas. When we put our forks into them, they were frozen on the inside. They told us the hiyakas were imported from Texas.

Ford Frick, the baseball commissioner, also made the trip. Years later, I saw him again when Elston represented the Yankees at one of the union negotiation meetings and asked me to go along. In one of the meetings I spoke up, saying how I thought the players were underpaid and mistreated. Frick looked at Elston and said, "I see you brought your secret weapon."

Shortly after the Yankees reported to spring training, Yogi and Elston posed for a picture in the *Sporting News* in which they were trading gloves. Everyone seemed certain that Elston would be the number-one catcher, except Casey. "I have to find out if Yogi can play right field and catch, too," said Casey. "I have to make up my mind about Elston

Howard. Do I drop him off the left-field platoon or do I go back to platooning him and letting Berra catch 125 games?"

Elston was a World Series hero, but he was still a second-class citizen at spring training. In St. Petersburg, the Chamber of Commerce welcomed the Yankees and St. Louis Cardinals with a breakfast at the Soreno Hotel. Elston was not invited, nor was he allowed to take a room there. Elston refused to spend another spring at the Williams' boardinghouse. Fortunately, he had met and befriended a young doctor who was actively fighting for civil rights: Ralph Wimbish. Dr. Wimbish and his family welcomed Elston into their home. Elston stayed there until he could find a place big enough for me and the kids when we came down later in the month. We also became good friends with Dr. Orion Ayer. He and his wife, Helen, were from St. Louis, and they made us feel right at home.

The 1959 season opened on April 12 at Yankee Stadium. The highlight of that cold day was the pregame ceremony in which Elston was presented the Babe Ruth Award before a crowd of 22,559. At the time, I thought Elston deserved the sports car. Elston did not play in the game; Yogi was the opening-day catcher. One day later, Elston made his season debut behind the plate in Baltimore, getting two hits in a 12–5 win over the Orioles.

A few days later, on April 18, Elston had one of his finest days as a hitter in Boston's Fenway Park. He had five singles in six at-bats during a 16–7 win over the Red Sox, collecting hits off Ted Bowsfield, Dick Sisler, Leo Kiely, and two off Bill Monbouquette. The very next day, Elston smashed a hard grounder over the head of Boston second baseman Pete Runnels. When Elston reached the bag, Runnels jokingly yelled over to first base, "All you need is a few more like that and you'll lead the league." Ted Williams had to be listening from right field. Leading the league would have been Elston's dream come true.

Elston got off to a hot start, but the Yankees did not. He was 10-for-20, but the Yankees had a 6–7 record. Soon after they had lost nine of the next ten games and were off to their worst early season record since 1940. Everything seemed to go wrong. Yogi's mother had her legs amputated and she died soon afterward. Mickey Mantle broke a finger. Andy Carey had hepatitis. Whitey Ford had elbow trouble. Ryne Duren was wild, walking eleven batters in 11⅔ innings. The infielders were making errors.

On May 7, the Yankees took a charter airplane from Kansas City to Los Angeles for an exhibition night game against the Dodgers. It was Roy Campanella Night. Campy was there in his wheelchair; it was the first time Elston had seen him since his terrible automobile accident after the 1957 season. I knew Campanella's wife, Ruthe, pretty well. Just before the accident, we knew Campy was going out with another woman and that he was going to divorce her. We heard that from Yvonne Crowe; George and Campy were very close friends. But Campy couldn't divorce her after the accident; it wouldn't have looked good. Though she stood by him all those years, Campy filed for separation in 1960 and eventually divorced her. Naturally the public was on his side, but Ruthe turned out to be the victim. If you ever wanted to start an argument between Elston and me, all you had to do was start talking about Campanella. Elston was on his side, and I would be on the other.

A crowd of 93,103—said to be the biggest ever to see a baseball game—turned out at the Coliseum and saw the Yankees win 6–2. Elston caught all nine innings and had two hits against a young left-hander named Sandy Koufax, who gave up eleven hits and five runs in 5⅓ innings.

By May 15, the Yankees were in seventh place at 11–15, five games behind the Cleveland Indians. On May 20, Frank Lary, the Detroit pitcher who had beaten the Yankees seven times in 1957, sent them into last place with a 13–6 loss at Yankee Stadium. With the Dodgers and Giants gone to California, the Yankees were the only game in town, and yet attendance was down. So were the team's spirits.

Elston cooled off, and his average sank into the .260s. "Our batting averages are sickly and sickening," Casey said. "It looks like we need a Ruth or a Cobb."

Instead, they got Hector Lopez. On May 26, the Yankees made another trade with Kansas City. John Kucks, Tom Sturdivant, and Jerry Lumpe were sent to the Athletics for pitcher Ralph Terry and Lopez, a black Panamanian outfielder who would be Elston's road roommate and good friend for the next five years. Looking back, it's hard to imagine that Elston and Hector were the only black players on the team.

Casey liked Hector, who also could play third base. "He hits the ball hard and plays the ball eagerly," Casey told the *Sporting News*. "He drives a ball into right field between the runners very well, even if he bats right-handed. He runs the bases like he meant it. In the field I would say he is adequate. No Pie Traynor maybe, but a game, battling ballplayer who appreciated the tremendous opportunity I am giving him."

The trade for Lopez and Terry helped a little. By June 12 the Yankees were 26–26, 3½ games behind the Chicago White Sox, a team that had been purchased during the off-season by Bill Veeck, the man who used to own the St. Louis Browns. On June 28, the Yankees lost a Sunday doubleheader in Chicago, 9–2, 4–2. The day before they had been beaten 5–4 on a grand slam by Suitcase Simpson. About a week later, the Yankees lost four straight games to Cleveland. Vic Power loved it; he homered in every game.

On June 18, Elston became a father for the third time when our daughter Karen was born two months prematurely. It was a very troubling time for us all. The doctor said there was a fifty-fifty chance of survival. He told us to go home and pray. They kept Karen in the hospital for about a month before we could bring her home.

When it came time for the All-Star Game, Elston was not named to the team. It didn't help that he had hurt his hand when he was hit by a pitch on June 25 in Kansas City and could not grip a bat. He missed a week. At the break he was hitting .273 with nine homers and 30 RBIs. Elston realized he had yet to become a full-time player, and his anxiety grew. For the first time, he spoke out publicly against Casey's platoon system. "I'm playing even less than I did a year ago, or so it seems," Elston said on July 29. "What disturbs me most is that I feel a hot streak coming on, but Casey seems fit to keep me on the bench. Playing a couple days, then sitting one or two out cools me off."

In one stretch, Elston homered in back-to-back games against Riverboat Smith of the Indians and Don Mossi of the Tigers. Yet he sat out the next day because Frank Lary was pitching. "I can hit righties as well as lefties," Elston said, "but how am I going to lift my average if I don't play?"

For the Yankees, the crusher came in early July. Playing at Fenway Park, they lost five straight games to the last-place Red Sox and fell out of the pennant race. In the final game of that series, a 5–3 loss, Elston was involved in a controversial play that involved umpire Nestor Chylak. Elston was playing first base when Boston's Don Buddin hit a slow infield roller with Sammy White on second base. The play at first was close, but Chylak called him safe. Elston couldn't believe it. As he turned to debate the call, White rounded third and headed for home. There was no throw. Elston was too busy arguing with Chylak.

The play caused a stir because the official scorer did not know how to rule it. American League president Joe Cronin was called in and he ruled that the play was a fielder's choice. "It's not an RBI or stolen base," Cronin said. "You can't charge an error to Howard because it was an error of omission."

By mid-August, the Yankees were twelve games behind the White Sox. Trade rumors began surfacing everywhere. One rumor had it that Yogi would be traded to the St. Louis Cardinals. Another had the Yankees trading off one of their pitchers for a young first baseman–outfielder named Willie McCovey. When the season ended, the Yankees were in third place with a 79–75 record, fifteen games behind the White Sox, who had won their first pennant since 1919. Elston finished the season with a .274 batting average, 18 home runs, and 73 RBIs in 442 at-bats. He played in 125 games. Yogi played in 131 games, batting .284 with 19 home runs and 69 RBIs in 472 at-bats. Mickey Mantle, who was booed throughout the season, finished at .285, with 31 home runs and 75 RBIs.

Trade rumors continued. The Yankees were trying to trade Gil McDougald; first to Washington for pitcher Camilo Pascual, then to Milwaukee for a young left-hander named Juan Pizarro. On December 20 the Yankees made a blockbuster deal, again with Kansas City—who else? This time they gave up Don Larsen, Norm Siebern, Marv Throneberry, and Hank Bauer for Joe DeMaestri, Kent Hadley, and outfielder Roger Maris.

A lot of the players became worried because they knew pay cuts were coming from George Weiss. When Elston got his contract in the mail, he was asked to take a $5,000 cut. "It was a good season," Elston told Dan Daniel in the *Sporting News*. "The front office insisted it had not come anywhere near expectations." Elston deliberately missed the start of spring training. He talked with Weiss about his salary, and it took a few days, but he eventually signed a contract for $25,500, a raise of $3,000.

In 1960, spring training came with optimism, even though the Yankees were now a third-place club fighting to recover from a dreadful season. "The Yankees can regain the pennant, their prestige, the world championship," Elston said. "The Yankee keys are a stronger Mantle, an uninjured Moose, better pitching, and Roger Maris proving himself to be a Yankee."

In the spring, Casey tried playing Maris in left field, with Hector Lopez in right to platoon with Yogi. But Hector had trouble, and Maris was returned to right field. On opening day in Boston on April 19, Roger batted leadoff and homered twice in an 8–4 win over the Red Sox. Elston batted seventh and went 1-for-4. He was sad to see Hank Bauer traded away in the Maris deal, but Maris and Elston became good friends over the next seven years. In the locker room, he took Bauer's stall, right next to Elston's.

Once again, it was thought that Elston would be the number-one catcher, but he got off to a slow start. On May 3, my birthday, he was hitting .205, with two home runs and nine RBIs. Yogi was playing right field, even some third base.

On May 18 Elston nearly came to blows with Jimmy Piersall, the emotionally challenged Cleveland outfielder. It all started when Yankee pitcher Duke Maas hit Cleveland pitcher Gary Bell with a pitch. Piersall was on deck and immediately started yelling at Elston, who was behind the plate. Elston got out of his crouch and made a move at Piersall, but umpire Al Smith held him back.

"Piersall accused me of giving the pitcher the sign to hit Bell," Elston said later. "He kept shouting, 'You'll be sorry for this. We'll get you in the head.' He wouldn't stop, so I went after him."

A few weeks later, the Indians put Piersall on the trading block and Casey was quoted as saying he wanted him on the Yankees. "Some people say this man is crazy," Stengel said. "Well, he certainly doesn't play crazy when he hits the ball. He never runs to third base."

Piersall was a nut. Everyone knew he was ill from the movie about his mental breakdown, "Fear Strikes Out." His behavior was beyond anything that baseball had ever seen. It all comes down to money. There is no penalty for terrible behavior as long as you draw fans in. There are lots of examples of that today. Look at Dennis Rodman, or Albert Belle. I read somewhere that Belle didn't know who Jackie Robinson was. Can you believe that?

On June 17 in Chicago a funny thing happened. Many of the Yankee players were infuriated by Chicago's new scoreboard that exploded with fireworks whenever a White Sox player would hit a homer. Poking fun at it, the Yankees, Elston included, decided to light sparklers in the dugout whenever a Yankee homered. That night, Clete Boyer and Mickey Mantle hit home runs and all the Yankees were waving sparklers, even Yogi, who was in the bullpen. That ticked off Bill Veeck, who one week later had some fireworks shipped to New York so that they could be shot off at Yankee Stadium whenever one of his players hit a home run. Veeck's plan didn't work. Dan Topping and George Weiss found out about it and called up the New York Fire Department, which cited a local law banning fireworks, and Veeck's plan was called off.

In late May the White Sox swept a three-game series from the Yankees. Mickey Mantle was slumping. Left field was still a sore spot in Casey's lineup. They were 19–19 on June 3. Elston was hitting .271 with four home runs and 22 RBIs. Things began to turn around shortly after Casey missed a week with a case of the flu. Ralph Houk managed the team in his absence and the Yankees started to win. Clete Boyer took over the job at third base. Andy Carey was traded to Kansas City for Bob Cerv. By June 24, the Yankees were 35–23.

In 1960, baseball decided to play two All-Star Games: one in Kansas City on July 11 and another in New York two days later. It was Frank Scott's idea to build up the pension. Players didn't have agents back then. Frank Scott was the players' union. For the third time in his career, Elston was named to the American League team. The players voted Yogi as the starting catcher even though Elston did most of the catching for the Yankees. Yogi was having a good year. He was hitting .291 at the All-Star break with eight home runs and 57 RBIs. Elston was hitting .255, with five home runs and 26 RBIs.

On July 31, Elston caught both games of a doubleheader against Kansas City and injured his left wrist while tagging out Bill Tuttle in a run-down. It was one of those injuries that can ruin your season, and it did. He missed a week; Yogi and John Blanchard did the bulk of the catching while he was out.

Elston came back on August 23 as the Yankees split a crucial two-game series at Chicago, losing the first game 5–1 and winning the second 3–2. In that series the "Go-Go" White Sox, a team that loved to run, failed to steal a base. Elston threw out three runners trying to steal, including Luis Aparicio twice. Starting on August 26, the Yankees played three doubleheaders in a row. They swept four games from Cleveland and split the other with Detroit. This gave the Yankees a four-game lead over Chicago heading into September.

The pennant that season didn't come easily. They needed a four-game sweep over Baltimore starting on September 15 to pull away. The Yankees, with a 97–57 record, barely beat out Chicago for the pennant. Elston played in 107 games, 91 of them at catcher, and batted .245 with six home runs and 36 RBIs. His fielding percentage was a respectable .987. Yogi, who caught in 63 games, batted .276 with 15 homers and 62 RBIs. Roger Maris was the American League Most Valuable Player with 39 home runs and 112 RBIs.

On September 28 in the last game of the season, Elston sprained a ligament in his right ring finger on a foul tip by Washington infielder Zoilo Versalles. Dr. Sidney Gaynor, the Yankee team doctor, said he would be limited to pinch-hitting duties until the World Series came to New York for Game 3 against the Pittsburgh Pirates.

Despite the doctor's orders, Elston got to play in Game 1. Pinch-hitting for Ryne Duren in the ninth inning with the Yankees losing 6–2, Elston blasted a mighty two-run homer off Elroy Face over the right-field screen at Forbes Field. It was his fourth World Series homer, but the Yankees lost 6–4. In Game 2, Elston ignited a seven-run sixth inning with a triple off the light tower in right field. He went 2-for-5 as the Yankees won 16–3. In New York for Game 3, Elston came up with the bases loaded in the first inning and hit a slow roller up the third-base line for an infield single. The next batter was Bobby Richardson, who belted a grand slam. Elston, who went 2-for-4, caught all nine innings as Whitey Ford pitched the Yankees to a 10–0 victory.

Casey benched Elston against Vernon Law in Game 4, and the Yankees lost 3–2. They also lost Game 5. Elston caught that game and went 1-for-3. Game 6 was particularly painful. Batting in the second inning off Bob Friend, a curveball broke the little finger on Elston's left hand. "Boy, was he annoyed," recalls Whitey Ford, who pitched a shutout that day. "He went right into the dugout. It was the only time I ever saw Ellie mad."

Elston had to go to the hospital. The doctor put his finger in a cast, and he was done for the Series. His batting average was .462. He could only sit in the dugout and watch the Yankees lose the seventh game, 10–9, on Bill Mazeroski's ninth-inning home run. Mickey Mantle cried. To Elston, it was a bad dream. The Yankees had outscored the Pirates 55–27 and somehow had lost the Series.

When Casey Stengel unexpectedly got fired a few days later, Elston had mixed emotions. He was always hot and cold about Casey. He respected him and his baseball knowledge, but by 1960 Stengel was seventy years old. In those later years Elston said Casey would fall asleep on the bench. As much as Elston respected Casey, he never did like sitting on the bench. Ralph Houk remembers one game where Casey goofed up. He sent Elston to bat as a pinch-hitter against a tough right-handed pitcher. "Elston was at the plate when Casey started yelling from the dugout, trying to call time out, but by then it was too late," Houk says. "Elston homered on the next pitch."

One week after Casey was fired, George Weiss was fired, too. Houk was named the new manager; Weiss was replaced by Roy Hamey. For Elston and the rest of the Yankees, it was a brand new ball game.

CHAPTER TEN

Baseball's Best Catcher

Ellie was a big reason why the '61 Yankees were one of the greatest teams ever.

—Tony Kubek

EXPLAINING RACIAL SEGREGATION TO YOUR FIVE-YEAR-OLD SON IS A very, very hard thing to do. When we would bring Elston Jr. down to spring training, Elston struggled to find the right words, the right way to tell our son about the difference between North and South, right and wrong, and black and white; that because of his skin color he had to use a different public rest room or was not allowed to eat a hamburger at certain restaurants. Beaches and swimming pools were off limits. "It's like a private club," Elston would say, "and we aren't members."

In the spring of 1961 Elston still was not allowed to stay with his teammates at the Soreno Hotel. Most Yankee stars did not stay at the team hotel. Players such as Mickey Mantle, Yogi Berra, and Whitey Ford were able to rent houses near the beach for their families. Elston wanted our kids to have a house near the beach too. He went to a few agencies and even got to look at a couple of places, but no one would rent to us. It didn't take long before he gave up the search.

Yes, it was the early 1960s, more than twelve years after Jackie Robinson had broken the color barrier, but black players still had to endure all sorts of indignities. On road trips around Florida, Elston and Hector Lopez had to sit inside the team bus and wait for their teammates to bring them sandwiches. Hector says one time the Yankees went to Fort Myers for a game and he and Elston had to stay overnight at a black funeral home with five dead bodies. "It was real quiet there," Hector said. "They didn't make much noise."

Dr. Ralph Wimbish, the local NAACP president in St. Petersburg, had seen and heard enough. Every year he had accepted the responsibility of finding suitable housing for the black ballplayers of the Yankees and St. Louis Cardinals. The teams took it for granted that Wimbish would find adequate housing in the black section of town for their few black players. Sometimes Dr. Wimbish had to bring Elston to his home on Fifteenth Avenue South and have him stay in the room of his young son. Later on, Elston and Hector were able to get a two-room apartment of their own, courtesy of Dr. Robert Swain, the local black dentist. "Since Negro players began coming here for spring training, the clubs would call on me to see that they got housed somewhere in the Negro district," Wimbish told Alex Haley, then a young writer for *Sport* magazine, that spring. "This year, before the teams came, the more I thought about it, the more I felt that it was a wrong which had gone on long enough. It was high time the clubs and the city put them in the hotel where they rightfully belonged with the rest of the players."

Wimbish had become quite vocal in his discontent. One day before spring camps opened, he drafted a letter to the Yankees and Cardinals. He finished it, but kept it in his car's glove compartment for a few days. A talk with Swain persuaded him to issue a public statement to the local newspaper, the *St. Petersburg Times*, announcing that he would no longer assist the Yankees or Cardinals in finding suitable housing for their black players. The teams would have to do it themselves, he said, and he dared them to pressure local hotels and businesses to stop segregation. Before the statement was published, Wimbish telephoned Elston in Teaneck early that February and warned him that a storm was brewing down South. "Look, I want to tell you about something before it happens, so you won't think it's anything personal," Wimbish said. Elston said he understood.

Dr. Wimbish's statement read: "Living conditions for the colored players in the Florida camps are not satisfactory . . . The Negro is not permitted the privacy of the white man . . . He is herded into a boarding house usually some distance from the center of town. There, he must answer the dinner bell and eat whatever is set on the table. He is not given an opportunity to fraternize with his white teammates."

Wimbish announced a boycott of Webb City, the largest department store in St. Petersburg, and other white businesses. Bill White remembers Wimbish's efforts fondly. "You know what we used to call him?" White asked. "We called him 'The Devil' because of all the hell he raised in behalf of the black ballplayers." For his efforts that spring, Wimbish received a number of death threats, and a cross was burned on his front yard.

Dr. Wimbish's home had a pool, which became like a social club for Elston and other black players such as Curt Flood, Bill White, George Crowe, Bob Gibson, Wes Covington, and Don Newcombe. There was one episode Elston told me about in which Swain came to Wimbish's house with a gun looking for Mrs. Swain because he had heard a rumor that she was sleeping with Curt Flood. (She was.) Elston was in bed when Dr. Wimbish knocked at the door and told Elston he needed to hide Mrs. Swain in the bedroom closet.

By 1961, the Yankees had two new black players on their roster: Jesse Gonder and Pedro Gonzalez. Through the media, Dan Topping, the co-owner of the Yankees, responded to Wimbish's letter: "We would like to have the whole team under one roof." Topping ordered Bob Fischel, the Yankees' head PR man, to talk with the local hotel officials and work things out. But Norville Smith, the manager of the Soreno, issued a statement of his own: "We hope to have [the Yankees] with us for many more years to come on the same basis." The "same basis," of course, meant that the black players would not be allowed inside his hotel.

Alex Haley wrote an article for *Sport* entitled "Baseball in a Segregated Town." Wendell Smith, the prominent black sportswriter for the *Pittsburgh Courier*, wrote a series of stories, and it didn't take long before the white sportswriters and wire services all joined in denouncing the shame.

Wrote Wendell Smith, "Cannot live with your teammates. Cannot enter the manager's hotel without special permission. Cannot enjoy any of the normal recreational facilities that white teammates enjoy. Quartered in a neighborhood where ordinarily you would be ashamed to be seen. Terribly embarrassed each day when the team's bus deposits you in 'Colored Town,' then proceeds to the plush hotel of your white teammates."

Said Wimbish, "You see, one of the best friends the Negro has today is publicity. Up until not too many years ago you wouldn't have known we existed from reading most newspapers. Under that quiet, the worst evils of prejudice went on and on and on, simply because nobody but Negroes really cared much about it. But now the publicity every day is forcing people to constantly really examine their consciences."

Bill White deserves a great deal of credit, too. The previous spring Bill had made some headlines when he sounded off to a St. Louis sportswriter about his frustrations with the housing situation in St. Petersburg. By the time Alex Haley spoke to him, White was a reluctant witness at the scene of the crime. Understandably, like most black players, he didn't want to be singled out as a spokesman or "troublemaker."

In 1960, Bill spoke out publicly against the St. Petersburg Yacht Club because it never invited black players to its weekly spring-training breakfasts. A white rookie could step off the bus and the very next day he would be invited to the Yacht Club. One year later, when the invitation finally came, Bill refused to go. "Why should I wake up at six in the morning to eat breakfast with a bunch of racists?" he reasoned.

Elston, too, was never invited to the Yacht Club breakfasts until that spring of '61. One day while Bill was eating breakfast in Mrs. Wimbish's kitchen he pleaded with Elston not to go. Elston didn't want to go, but someone from the front office, probably Dan Topping, called and insisted that he attend. Because he was a New York Yankee, Elston felt obligated. So he went. Soon after, Elston began to speak out publicly, too. He called Frank Scott, the general representative of what later became the Major League Players Association, and demanded that they take action against owners who condoned spring-training discrimination. Elston was told the topic would be put on the agenda for the association's meeting that July.

Black players on other teams in Florida began to complain too. The Milwaukee Braves trained in Bradenton, about thirty-five miles south of St. Petersburg. When Birdie Tebbetts, the manager, was quoted in the *Sporting News* as saying his black players were content staying at a rooming house instead of the team hotel, two of his best players, Henry Aaron and Wes Covington, took exception.

"Sometimes the place is so crowded that they have two guys sleeping in the hall," Aaron told the *Sporting News* that spring. "They have five guys living in two rooms. They put two beds in one room, two more in the hall and another bed in a smaller room. They got a room in the garage. They call it the penthouse. At the most you could put four people in there and they have eight. They said this place was carefully selected for us. Carefully selected for what?"

Back in New York, Dan Topping was under fire. The media began accusing the Yankee ownership of putting up a lukewarm fight in behalf of their black players. Topping's excuse was that the contracts were signed with the hotels before spring training. Eventually, Topping said the Yankees would investigate the possibility of finding a new spring-training base. As it turned out, Topping owned a winter home in Fort Lauderdale and began to entertain offers from city officials there who promised a new ballpark. C. H. Alberding, the owner of the Soreno and the Vinoy Park, where the Cardinals stayed, issued a statement from Tulsa, Oklahoma: "If they insist, the Yankees and Cardinals can look elsewhere."

The furor refused to go away and became too embarrassing for a high-profile team such as the Yankees, who decided they would rather run than fight. Since 1926 they had called St. Petersburg their spring home. In 1962, that home would be Fort Lauderdale.

August Busch, owner of the Cardinals, decided to stay, but he had other worries. Blacks, like whites, drank beer. What if his black customers decided on a Budweiser boycott? Bad publicity out of Florida would not be good for his business. So the Cardinals decided to stay in St. Pete, but only after they were able to buy a local hotel, the Outrigger Inn, where they could house all their players.

That last spring in St. Petersburg was the first under new manager Ralph Houk and new general manager Roy Hamey, who years earlier had been one of George Weiss's assistants. As much as Elston respected Casey Stengel, he found Houk to be more approachable, a former catcher who would listen. Best of all, he no longer had to put up with Casey's platoon system. There would be no more games in the outfield. Houk loved Elston's attitude, the way he handled pitchers, and his rifle-like arm. After Elston threw out all seven runners who tried to steal on him that spring, Houk assured him he was the Yankees' number-one catcher. Now it was Yogi's turn to play some left field. As usual, the Yankees were well blessed behind the plate. There was Yogi, now thirty-five years old, and Johnny Blanchard, a left-handed hitter with power. Most teams were lucky to have one good catcher who could also hit. The 1961 Yankees had three who combined for more than sixty home runs.

Elston's hand, broken in Game 6 of the 1960 World Series, was completely healed. His contract for 1961 called for him to make $29,000, a raise of $3,500. Until that spring Elston had hit from a wide-open batting stance much like Joe DiMaggio's. Wally Moses, the new hitting coach, worked on changing that. He got Elston to close his stance. Wally reshaped it so that his feet were much closer together, with the left foot extended far ahead of his right one. Elston said these changes made him "a real hitter."

Elston figured something had to be done about his hitting. After batting .314 in 1958, his average had slipped to .273 in 1959 and .245 in 1960. All those long fly balls to "death valley" in left field were killing his average, and he was embarrassed by the dip in his power numbers. "That good year spoiled me," he told the *Sporting News*. "I hit that good average with a wide spread stance. I also was trying to pull every pitch to left field. . . . With the new stance I have been able to hit the ball much better through the middle and to the opposite field."

The 1961 season will always be remembered as the year of the hitter. It was an expansion season with two new teams, the Los Angeles Angels and the new Washington Senators—the old Senators had moved to Minnesota—joining the American League. The pitching, to be kind, wasn't as good. The Yankees hit 240 home runs that season, setting a major-league record.

Blessed with a talented ball club considered by some to be the best team of all time, Ralph Houk was in a good situation, but his biggest problem was what to do with his three catchers. "Well, right in the first month of the season, [Hector] Lopez slumped a bit, so I sent Yogi to the outfield and he fit right in. Before that he had been alternating with Howard. Behind the plate, after that, the catching sorta molded itself.

"I caught Howard most of the time. I caught Blanchard against certain pitchers and in certain ballparks and didn't catch Howard in doubleheaders. He's only caught doubleheaders against left-handed pitchers. This kept Howard strong and kept Blanchard sharp for pinch-hitting. We started winning that way, and that's the thing we're interested in. It's unusual for a manager to have this kind of problem—three fine catchers with good bats—which I consider a nice problem."

The Yankees got off to a decent start. Between June 5 and August 6 Blanchard's clutch hitting won or tied eight games for the Yankees. Five of those clutch hits were home runs. As a result, Blanchard got more playing time, and Elston played less against right-handers. After the first week in June, Elston was hitting .389 and yet had only 90 at-bats. Nobody knew it then, but it might have cost him a chance to win the batting title.

Said Houk, "I said I had three number-one catchers at the beginning of the year and that I also considered them my bench. I told them that the fella who was doing the best—the man with the hot bat—would be doing most of the catching." The problem was that he had three hot bats.

On June 5 against Chicago, Houk let Elston play the entire series. He caught Friday, Saturday, and a doubleheader on Sunday. Chuck Stobbs, a tough lefty, was to pitch the nightcap.

"Are you tired?" Houk asked.

"Who's tired when you're hitting good?" Elston replied.

"Fine," said Houk. "You'll catch that one, too."

Elston did, and he went 3-for-4.

On June 25 against the Twins, Elston had a three-run homer and a run-scoring single in an 8–5 win. Afterward, reporters, looking to stir up some controversy, tried to bait him into criticizing Houk about his playing time.

"He's helped me plenty," said Elston of Houk. "He's a quiet man and he talks things over with you. If he's got something to say he tells you nice and quiet-like, and the next thing you know you're talking it over.

"He's telling me to hit the ball through the middle. Like that. He can tell when I'm rolling my wrists too much and trying to kill everything to left field. He notices things like that."

On May 21 Elston was ejected from a game for the first and only time in his major-league career. In the third inning of a nationally televised game, Rollie Sheldon was pitching to Kansas City's Whitey Herzog when Elston began questioning umpire John Rice about his strike zone. "What did you call that?" Elston said as he began to turn around.

"Don't turn around; you know what I called it," Rice replied.

Elston turned around and said, "I still want to know what you called that." Rice ejected him right away. Rice later said Elston was "delaying the game." He also said Elston used some bad words. Bobby Richardson later recalled, "I can assure you that if Elston ever argued with the umpire, the umpire was wrong."

The ejection didn't prevent Elston from being named to the American League All-Star team. Because Yogi was named the starting catcher, Elston played outfield in the game, but it was becoming apparent that Elston was the best defensive catcher in baseball. Luis Aparicio, the Chicago White Sox speedster, was the first player to lead the American League in stolen bases for six consecutive years. That season, Elston had his number. Against the Yankees one day in June, Aparicio led off with a single and two pitches later took off for second. Elston sprang up like a jack-in-the-box and fired a strike to Richardson, who easily tagged him out. The next day, Aparicio singled again to lead off the game; moments later Elston threw him out again!

By July the Yankees were in a pennant race with Detroit, and Elston was chasing Detroit's Norm Cash for the batting title. On July 7, Elston hit two homers in a 4–0 win over Cleveland and apologized afterward. "I didn't mean to hit the homers and I didn't know how I did it," he said. Elston had not homered until June 14, and now he had four. He was trying to hit everything up the middle. At this point the Yankees had a 50–28 record and the Detroit Tigers were 52–29.

In Chicago on July 13 Elston homered onto the left-field roof at Comiskey Park. "I honestly didn't try to hit a home run," he said. "I gave that up at the start of the season. I guess it is true that if you meet the pitch, the homers will come."

On July 28, a freak accident knocked Elston out of the lineup. When catching, Elston always liked to get as close to home plate as he could. But in a game against Chicago, he had to leave in the third inning when he was struck in the right rear side by the backlash of Floyd Robinson's bat. Elston came back the next day, but he never backed away from the plate.

By early August, the baseball world was talking about the home-run race between Roger Maris and Mickey Mantle. Elston's locker was right next to Maris's, and every day he would just smile as the press asked Roger the same questions over and over again. While the M & M boys were being hounded, hardly anyone paid much attention to the batting race. By August 5, Elston had 262 at-bats, 16 walks, and two sacrifices, for 280 plate appearances. With 56 games left, he needed to have four plate appearances in each game to reach the 504 needed to qualify for a batting title. Because of expansion, the minimum number of plate appearances had gone up from 477 to 502. Only six Yankees had ever won batting crowns. No American League catcher had ever won a batting championship. Only two National League catchers had won one—Ernie Lombardi in 1942 and Gene Hargrove in 1926.

Elston thought he could catch Cash. "I think I can do it. But I don't know if I can get enough base hits to win it even if I get enough [at-bats]." Ten days later, he changed his mind. "No, I don't think I can qualify," he said. "If you look back, not too many catchers have won the batting title. Houk's not going to switch me around just to win one. We're interested in winning the pennant. I haven't played enough games this year."

On August 6, 1961, the Yankees beat Minnesota 7–6 in fifteen innings. Elston doubled off Pedro Ramos in the second inning. In the fourth he singled to left center. In the fifth he lined a single off Ramos's glove and Ramos had to leave the game. It was his sixth hit in seven at-bats and eighth in his last eleven. In the seventh inning he struck out. In the tenth he grounded out. In the eleventh he singled; he struck out in the fourteenth. And he caught every inning.

On August 19, the Yankees and Indians were tied 2–2 when Billy Gardner doubled. Maris and Mantle made outs and Yogi was walked intentionally to get to Elston. Elston made them pay with a single to right center to secure Whitey Ford's twenty-first win. "Maybe they don't know I'm hitting the ball this year," Elston joked afterward.

On September 1, the Tigers came to town for a big showdown, trailing the Yankees by 1½ games. In the first game of a doubleheader, with runners on first and third and two outs, Elston raced back and reached far into the seats to catch Norm Cash's foul pop in the eighth inning of a scoreless game. In the ninth, left-hander Don Mossi got Maris and Mantle out. But Elston singled to right center and scored the winning run on singles by Berra and Skowron. Elston went 0-for-4 in the nightcap, but the Yankees won 7–2. In the next game, the score was tied at 5–5 in the ninth. Batting against Ron Kline with two runners on and two out, Elston missed the first pitch, but he got the next one. It was his fifteenth homer of the season.

Elston finished the year with a .348 batting average, 155 hits, 21 home runs, and 77 RBIs. In 129 games, he had only 490 at-bats. Norm Cash won the batting title at .361.

I saw the Billy Crystal movie *61**, and I liked it a lot. Much of it was true about there being people in New York who were booing Roger and pulling for Mickey. The movie even had an actor, Bobby Hosea, playing Elston, but he didn't have much of a speaking role. Only once was it mentioned that Elston was hitting .340.

The Yankees won 110 games that season and beat the Cincinnati Reds in five games in the World Series. Elston was a hero in Game 1 when he broke up a scoreless game with a solo homer off Jim O'Toole in the fourth inning of a 2–0 victory pitched by Whitey Ford. The home run, his fifth in World Series play, was the first home run O'Toole had allowed in sixteen games, a span covering 108 innings. Elston caught all five games in the Series, picking up five hits in twenty at-bats.

By now a lot of people knew what we already knew: Elston was the best catcher in baseball.

CHAPTER ELEVEN

Teaneck

I've got my wife and kids to think about. The better catcher I get to be, the better I'll be able to provide for them.
                                                    —ELSTON HOWARD, 1962

WHEN HE CAME HOME TO ST. LOUIS, ELSTON'S BIG SMILE WOULD always light up the town. He enjoyed the occasional visits back home, and no trip was more eventful than the one he made in February 1962, when he was honored as the St. Louis Man of the Year.

The *Sporting News* threw a big testimonial dinner at the Jefferson Hotel, and it seemed like half the town was there that night: Elston's mother, cousins, his coaches from Vashon High School, Wendell Hill and some of Elston's other old school buddies. Coming off his finest season in the majors, Elston was the toast of the town. A local reporter asked Elston about the award. "What does it signify?" Elston looked over at Teannie Edwards, his sandlot coach and mentor, standing nearby and said, "Work hard, keep your mouth shut, and mind your own business." That was Teannie's motto.

Elston was about to begin his eighth year with the Yankees, and now he truly was one of the team's stars. Fort Lauderdale had replaced St. Petersburg as the team's spring base after all the fuss the year before concerning segregated housing. Fort Lauderdale, just north of Miami, was much more tolerant to integration than St. Petersburg.

In Fort Lauderdale, the Yankees had a hotel where all their players were welcomed. Aptly, it was called the Yankee Clipper. In Fort Lauderdale we could go to the white shopping centers, we could drink at the white water fountains, use the white bathrooms, eat in the white restaurants. At first we were a bit apprehensive, and it made me mad to think what we had gone through for all those years in St. Petersburg. In fact, it took some adjustment on our part. Often when we would go out to dinner, our friends would call ahead just to make sure the restaurants would serve blacks. One time, I was walking past the hotel coffee shop when Paul Grossinger, the owner of the Catskills resort, saw me and motioned for me to come join him. At first I hesitated. It had become a reflex; I had to think about it before I walked in.

Sometimes the racism got to be funny. One night when young pitcher Al Downing and Elston went out to dinner, they were standing outside the hotel lobby when a man drove up in a Cadillac. The man got out of his car, looked at Al, and tossed him the keys.

Al Downing spent seven seasons as Elston's roommate on road trips. Elston liked him and thought he had the talent to be a great pitcher. "He's got fire in his arm," Elston would say. As roommates they got along quite well. By day, Al was a very quiet young man who loved to read all kinds of books and take frequent naps. Elston used to think he had some sort of sleeping disease. He could sleep anywhere. By night, he sometimes made Elston mad by sneaking girls up to the room. Elston would get furious whenever Al made him wait outside.

Years later, Al said he learned a lot from the time he spent with Elston. "I would follow him around like a little puppy," Downing recalled. "Every night we would sit in the room and talk about baseball. Talk about pitching, talk about hitters. He would tell me the key to winning in the majors was to think for myself. He told me never be afraid of shaking him off." Because of Elston, Downing learned how to become a pitcher. Elston encouraged him to throw the slider on 3-and-2, and throw it with confidence. Al always had talent, but he had some tough luck, too. One teammate said, "he was so good, he had enough talent to pitch a no-hitter and lose."

Elston loved life on the road, Downing said. Elston would always get up early in the morning with the sunrise. No matter which town they were in, Elston would know where all the fruit stands were and would walk there every morning. Elston loved his steak dinners, but breakfast was something special. He loved fruit and kept his room well stocked with apples, pears, bananas. The fruit-stand guys in every American League city got to know him pretty well.

Detroit was one of Elston's favorite towns. There was a Coney Island hot-dog stand near the ballpark that Elston just loved to death. As soon as the team bus pulled up to the hotel, zoom, Elston was out of the door.

Oh, he loved those chili dogs. He'd go there and buy five, sometimes six of them in a paper bag and bring them back to his room.

When it came to shopping, Elston was the team leader. Every road trip he knew where all the clothing stores were, and he'd bring along an empty suitcase to bring it all home. He'd load up on ties, jackets, shirts. And he would always buy gifts for everyone in our family, particularly our daughter Karen.

Elston always tried to bring something home for Karen. About a year after she was born, we began to notice that something was wrong with her. She was not able to sit up. We took her to doctor after doctor but none of them ever told us exactly what was wrong. Finally, we took her to Dr. Sidney Gaynor, the Yankees' team doctor. We always liked him because he was always very blunt. He came right out and told us what we had to know. She had cerebral palsy.

We were taken by surprise. I didn't know anything about cerebral palsy. I had to get an encyclopedia to find out what it was. Our child would grow up with a brain disorder that affected her muscles and her coordination. Right away Elston decided that no matter the cost, Karen would have the best treatment available. Over the years we became very involved with the local cerebral palsy group. When Karen got older, we joined an organization known as New Horizons whose purpose was to benefit the retarded. We helped them raise thousands of dollars through benefits and a golf tournament in Elston's name. We gave Karen everything we could give. Most of all, we gave her our love.

Elston's 1962 contract arrived in the mail. He was given a $13,500 raise. After batting .348 and playing well in his sixth World Series, he was now making $42,500, making him, a six-time All-Star, one of the higher-paid players in baseball.

Ralph Houk was always very proud of his catching corps. Elston, Yogi, and John Blanchard accounted for sixty-four homers in 1961. "You've got Howie back there and you've got to play him," Houk boasted. "Who's better? He hit .348 last year. How many catchers hit .348 in this business?" As usual, the Yankees were expected to win another American League championship in 1962, and Whitey Ford was one of the main reasons why. Elston loved catching Whitey, who had won twenty-five games in 1961, and they developed a special relationship. Elston used to say he could catch Whitey "in a rocking chair." Not too many people know that it was Elston who first labeled Whitey "Chairman of the Board."

Elston's favorite radio station was WNEW, a local AM station in New York that had a disc jockey named William B. Williams. Elston met him at a dinner one night and the two became friends. On the radio, Williams often played Frank Sinatra records and often referred to him as "chairman of the board." And so that spring, when writers started asking Elston how good Whitey was, Elston had nothing but praise.

"You know people rave about all the guts Whitey has, what a great guy he is in the clutch and how he never beats himself," Elston said. "That's right, all those things are true. But what burns me up is that not enough folks really know the real reason he's a great pitcher, and I'll tell anybody in one word—stuff!

"You know what? He works a game so good, he doesn't need a catcher," Elston said. "He's just chairman of the board."

Whitey always loved his title. Chairman of the Board was written on the plaque they dedicated to him in the outfield section of Yankee Stadium that is called Monument Park. Said Whitey, "If that was true, that Ellie was saying I was to pitching what Frank Sinatra was to singing, I am very flattered."

By now, Elston was the best catcher in baseball. Luis Aparicio and Zoilo Versalles, the speediest runners in the American League, had trouble running on Elston. Nobody dared run on him unless they got a good jump on the pitcher.

No one else had an arm like Elston's, or a reputation to match. There's a story that Bobby Richardson tells about Versalles. Apparently, as a rookie, Versalles had heard how tough it was to run on Elston. One day he took a lead and Whitey Ford threw to first base to pick him off. Versalles just kept his head down and took off for second and was thrown out by ten feet. After his slide, he got up, dusted himself off and said to Bobby Richardson, "That Howard, he's got some arm."

But there was more to catching than just having a strong arm. Elston had the smarts to call a game. He kept a book in his mind on how to pitch certain hitters. Pitchers found it easy to trust his judgment. Every spring training, Elston worked for hours with coach Jim Hegan on blocking low pitches in the dirt. He became so good at it that at times he would instruct his pitchers to throw their two-strike pitches in the dirt. "Don't worry," he told them. "I'll dig it up."

Ralph Terry was always impressed. "Everybody knows the pitcher throws the ball, but in the case of Elston Howard, you've got a catcher who does more than what is expected of him," he said in 1962. "Ellie does the extra stuff. Howard's a great catcher. He is one of the best I've ever seen. He's just about psychic behind the plate. He thinks with the pitcher. He's got that wonderful sense of knowing just what ought to be thrown in any given situation. You seldom see a pitcher shake Howard off. If he wants something, I go with him."

In 1962, Elston had three homers in his first thirteen games as the Yankees got off to a 12–6 start. On May 2, he belted a two-run homer in the ninth inning off Joel Horlen to give the Yankees a 4–3 win over the White Sox. By June 8, the Yankees were 29–10 and Elston had seven homers, 31 RBIs, and a .265 batting average. On June 15, the Yankees went into Cleveland for a four-game series and got swept. Elston went 3-for-12 for the weekend. When the series ended in a 6–3 loss, Elston had caught thirty-two straight games. On June 19 Houk finally gave him a day off. Never did Elston complain. He had waited all of his Yankee career to be an everyday player. Now, he expected to play every day.

A few days later, on June 24, Elston got another day off as the Yankees finished up a weekend series in Detroit. With Frank Lary on the mound, a pitcher whose lifetime record against the Yankees was 28–10, Houk gave Yogi Berra the start. The game lasted seven hours and Yogi caught all twenty-two innings. Elston's only appearance came as a pinch-hitter; he grounded out batting for Marshall Bridges in the seventh inning.

On June 30, Elston, batting .267 with seven homers and 34 RBIs, was named to the American League All-Star team along with fellow catchers Sherm Lollar of the White Sox and Earl Battey of the Twins. At the All-Star break, the Yankees were 46–34 and Cleveland was 48–36. The Yankees were winning, but they couldn't pull away. On August 19, in 102-degree heat in Kansas City, Elston hit two three-run homers. For the day he went 4-for-6 and drove in eight runs in a 21–7 victory over the Athletics. "My number-one all-time day," he called it. In one day, Elston's batting average went from .270 to .280, still a far cry from the .348 he had hit in 1961. "I've got to go big the last six weeks of the season to come anywhere near last year," he said.

In that same game Mickey Mantle drove in seven runs. Mantle would be the American League MVP that year, but Elston's late-season production helped the Yankees win the American League flag. It didn't come easily. In late August the Yankees lost six straight games and saw their lead shrink to two games over the Twins. But behind the pitching of Ford and Terry, the team righted the ship and clinched the pennant on September 25 with an 8–3 win at Washington. After the game, Elston, Yogi, and a few other veteran players shunned the usual champagne celebration to watch the heavyweight fight between Sonny Liston and Floyd Patterson on TV. Elston loved boxing. He was surprised when Patterson got knocked out in the first round.

The Yankees finished 96–66. Whitey Ford won 17 games and Ralph Terry won 18. Roger Maris had only 33 homers, not 61. Elston played a career-high 136 games and hit .279 with 21 home runs and 91 RBIs in 494 at-bats. The Yankees had to wait to find out who would be their National League opponent in the World Series. The Giants and Dodgers had tied for first place and needed a three-game playoff to determine a champion. When the Giants won the third game, we began packing our bags for San Francisco. My sister Loyette lived there, and we stayed with her instead of at the team hotel. San Francisco was one of our favorite cities. We loved the cosmopolitan atmosphere, the Fisherman's Wharf area, and all those nice restaurants. It was to be Elston's seventh World Series, and it was the first time Elston and Willie Mays had played against each other since the days when we were in Puerto Rico in 1955. After the first day of workouts at Candlestick Park, Elston saw Willie. "How do you put up with the wind?" he asked. Mays replied, "If you think this is bad, wait until it shifts directions."

In Game 1, the wind was a factor. Whitey Ford, the starting pitcher, was working on a record that still stands today—he had pitched thirty-three scoreless innings in World Series play. But the Giants had no problem hitting Whitey's pitches. When they roughed him up for runs in the second and third innings, it didn't take Elston long to determine what was wrong. "Whitey wasn't the pitcher I know early in the game," Elston said afterward. "He has a big curveball, you know, but it was breaking just about four inches, like a little wrinkle."

The wind was blowing so hard, it was taking the bite out of his curveball. In the fourth inning Elston sat next to Whitey in the dugout and told him to junk the pitch. Whitey went to the slider the rest of the way and the Giants didn't score again. Once again, Elston was a World Series hero. He had two hits, the second off Stu Miller to drive in the final run in a 6–2 victory. He also scored a big run in the eighth. The Yankees were ahead 4–2 when Elston slid into third base on Dale Long's RBI single. When Clete Boyer hit a fly ball to shallow left field, Elston saw shortstop Jose Pagan retreat to make the catch, instead of left fielder Felipe Alou, and alertly tagged up and raced home. Elston was not the fastest man on the field, just one of the smartest.

Elston hurt his wrist on the slide into third base. He was a late scratch for Game 2. With Elston having trouble gripping the bat, the Yankees went with Yogi against Jack Sanford, a tough right-hander. The Yankees lost that one, 2–0.

Elston returned for Game 3 in New York and caught Bill Stafford's four-hitter in a 4–2 victory in front of a Yankee Stadium crowd of 71,434. Elston went 1-for-3 but was robbed of a home run when Felipe Alou made a good catch in front of the left-field stands. The Yankees split the two remaining games in New York, meaning we had to return to San Francisco. When we got back to Loyette's house, that's when the rain came. It poured for four straight days, and each day Game 6 was postponed. It drove Elston nuts. When the Series resumed, the Yankees lost 5–2. That set up Game 7, which the Yankees won 1–0. Ralph Terry was the hero that day, teaming up with Elston to pitch a four-hitter. In the ninth inning, with Willie Mays on third base, Willie McCovey at the plate, and Orlando Cepeda on deck, Elston knew Terry had to pitch carefully. He called for a fastball, and McCovey hit a rocket—right into Bobby Richardson's glove. The Yankees were champions again.

Offensively, it was not one of Elston's best World Series. He batted only .143, but no one in the Yankee lineup hit their weight. Mickey Mantle batted .120, Roger Maris .174, Bill Skowron .222. The Yankees hit just three home runs, and yet they had won again, this time with pitching.

Each Yankee player collected a winner's share of $10,987. Back then, that was a lot of money, and it helped us decide to buy a bigger house. It was definitely time. With three kids, the house on Howland Avenue was too small, so we began to look around. I wanted to move somewhere else, but Elston loved Teaneck, so naturally that's where we looked first. We went to a real estate agent who showed us a vacant lot on Edgemont Place in the most affluent section of town. All the houses were big, and the streets were wide and lined with trees. The elementary school was two blocks away.

Our lawyer, Leonard Stone, warned us, though. He said that once the owner found out a black family was going to buy it, he wouldn't sell it to us. We found some builders and gave them the money to buy the lot. Next we found an architectural firm, Hanson and Hanson. They drew up some sketches for us. We decided to go with a two-story colonial. Mal Goode, the renowned *Pittsburgh Courier* writer who later worked at the United Nations, bought our house on Howland Avenue.

As it turned out, our lawyer was right in warning us of problems. We had the property, but the architect kept asking where it was. When we finally told him, he went immediately to the mayor, Matty Feldman. Mayor Feldman came to visit us one evening that fall just before work was to start on the house. We had met him before, back in the spring when the city of Teaneck held a ceremony at city hall and called it "Elston Howard Day." On that day, Mayor Feldman gave Elston the keys to the city. Now he was in our home trying to take them away.

CHAPTER TWELVE

MVP

*One of these days, I want baseball fans to mention my name in the
same breath as Yogi Berra and Roy Campanella.*
—ELSTON HOWARD, 1963

MAYOR FELDMAN DIDN'T COME TO OUR HOME TO THREATEN US. ACTU-
ally he was very cordial, very polite, but his message was clear: Please don't
build that house on Edgemont Place. As mayor of Teaneck, he came to
tell us about another lot in the nearby West Englewood section of town,
one that was "nicer" and "bigger" than the one we intended to build on in
Teaneck. Our lawyer, Leonard Stone, told us that a group of our would-be
neighbors had held a meeting. In no uncertain terms, they told the mayor
to do whatever it took to keep us out of their neighborhood.

Of course, I was furious about the whole thing. My husband was the
first-string catcher for the New York Yankees. We were a good family
with three good kids. Who were these people, these underlings—I used
to call them "truck drivers"—to pass judgment on us?

Still, there was never any doubt about what we had to do. We were
moving to Edgemont Place. The price tag, I think, was fifty thousand
dollars. While the house was being built over the spring and summer of
1963, somebody came onto our property and spray-painted and carved
racial epithets on the inside walls and on the porch. It cost us a lot of
money to have it cleaned up. Later, when we had moved in that fall, some
of our new neighbors were not friendly at all. Some gave us the silent

treatment. Others were very kind—the Moores across the street, and the Goldclangs next door.

Work began on the house just as Elston left for spring training in Fort Lauderdale. The Yankees had essentially the same team that had won its second straight World Championship in 1962, except that Bill Skowron had been traded to the Los Angeles Dodgers. Moose was one of Elston's best friends going back to the days when they played for the Kansas City Blues in 1953. It was never good to see anyone get traded, particularly one of your friends. In retrospect, Moose's trade was no big surprise. He was having problems at home with his wife, and the Yankees had Joe Pepitone coming up.

Elston always would tell me how Joe Pepitone wasted his talent, and Joe would be the first to agree. "Ellie would take me aside and tell me about how much potential I had," Pepitone recalls. "He told me not to waste it and that he would never let me forget it. He would always point to my flaws and get on my case. He was one of the real leaders on that club. He was that type of guy, one of the best I ever played with."

Elston, now thirty-four years old, was ready to begin his ninth season in the majors. His lifetime average was .285. He had 100 home runs and 467 RBIs. Now he was determined to have his finest year ever. "Let's say I hope to hit .300 or better," he told writers that spring. "I will be happy if I knock in 85–90 runs and hit 25 home runs. I don't think I've reached my peak yet."

Like many people, we were surprised when we heard the news about Marshall Bridges. In 1963 he was a thirty-one-year-old relief pitcher from Mississippi, and he got shot in the left leg one night in a local nightclub just as spring training was about to begin. Elston liked Marshall and thought he was a good pitcher, but, thank goodness, Elston always kept his distance. I remember eating dinner with Marshall once in the Yankee dining room at Fort Lauderdale. They had all sorts of steaks, chops, lobsters, anything you wanted. Marshall, however, wanted nothing to do with it. "I can't eat this," he said. "It's gonna make me sick." We laughed when he got up from the table and said, "Man, I gotta go out and find some real soul food."

Elston liked another young pitcher that spring. But years later, Elston never forgave Jim Bouton for the things he said in that book he wrote, and I never did either. Talk about a lack of gratitude! It was Elston who helped turn him into a twenty-game winner. Like he did with Whitey Ford, Elston gave Bouton a nickname. He called him "Bulldog." "He's got it here, in the heart," said Elston. "He's just like a bulldog, a battling kind of a bulldog." Said Clete Boyer, "Bouton always wanted to take Whitey Ford's spotlight. He couldn't do it. He was a punk, but he was a good pitcher."

Once again, the Yankees were favored to win the American League. Back in those days, that's what we expected. Thanks to Elston having one of his most productive seasons, the Yankees won easily. In fact, Elston was named the league's Most Valuable Player. Being the first black man to win this award in the American League was quite an honor. It was Elston who carried the team offensively when Mickey Mantle and Roger Maris got hurt and missed most of the season. By May 5, Elston had hit three of his first six homers to right field. He was using heavier bats, some weighing as much as thirty-eight ounces. With that familiar closed stance, he began taking full advantage of the short porch in right field. "The heavier the bat, the less chance you have of overswinging and looking foolish at the plate," he said after he hit two homers off left-hander Jim Kaat in a 3–2 win at Minnesota.

Game after game Elston came up with clutch hits. Dick Radatz, the Boston relief pitcher, called Elston "the toughest hitter in the Yankee lineup." On April 19, Elston's home run off Al Duckworth broke up a 3–3 tie in the ninth inning at Washington. On May 12 he doubled in the decisive run off Steve Barber in a 2–0 win at Baltimore. On May 15 at Minnesota, he drove in the winning run with a single off Ray Moore. On May 31 he hit a two-run homer off Mudcat Grant in a 4–0 win over Cleveland.

On June 5 Mickey Mantle, chasing after a Brooks Robinson home run, crashed into a fence at Baltimore and broke his foot. Mantle played in only sixty-five games that season. Maris, hobbled by leg injuries, played in only ninety. With Mantle out of the lineup, Ralph Houk made Elston the Yankees' cleanup hitter against left-handed pitching. Against right-handers, he usually batted fifth, sometimes sixth.

By June 16, Elston had twelve homers and was among the league leaders, behind Bob Allison and Dick Stuart. The Yankees were in first place, 4½ games ahead of the White Sox. On June 23, Elston was named to the American League All-Star team for the seventh time. On June 29 his home run off Chet Nichols gave the Yankees a 2–0 win at Fenway Park. On July 4 he homered off Chicago's Gary Peters in a 9–1 win. On July 11 at Los Angeles, his tenth-inning single gave the Yankees a 3–2 win over Julio Navarro (father of current major-league pitcher Jaime Navarro). Three days later he drove in three runs with a double and homer in a 5–0 win at Kansas City.

On July 21, Elston hit his twenty-first homer, matching his season total from the previous two years. "I'd like to beat the American League record for catchers," he declared that day. The American League record was thirty, shared by Gus Triandos and Yogi Berra, who had become a Yankee coach and part-time player. The National League record was forty-one, held by Roy Campanella.

The Yankees went 22–9 in July, and by the time Mantle returned to the lineup on August 4, the Yankees had a 10½-game lead. On August 11, with the Yanks trailing the Angels 4–1 with two out and two on in the ninth inning, Elston delivered a game-tying homer. On August 25, he homered twice off Juan Pizarro in a 4–0 win over the White Sox.

Baseball writers began taking note and promoted Elston as an MVP candidate. When the season ended, the Yankees had won 104 games. Elston, admittedly pressing for the home-run record, finished with 28 homers, 85 RBIs, and a .528 slugging percentage, fourth best in the league. His fielding percentage, .994, was the best among baseball catchers. He won the Gold Glove.

For the eighth time in his career, Elston was playing in the World Series. Unfortunately, the Yankees took on the Dodgers, who swept them in four straight games. Elston and several of his teammates got angry when he read that one writer in Los Angeles had called them "the Mets in pinstripes." To the Yankees, that was an insult.

Sandy Koufax, the National League's Most Valuable Player, beat them in the first game 5–2 at Yankee Stadium (in 1963, both league MVPs wore number 32 on their uniforms). At one stretch Koufax retired fourteen batters in a row until Elston singled to right field in the fifth inning. Koufax set a World Series record with fifteen strikeouts, but he only got Elston once, swinging in the seventh inning.

Al Downing was the losing pitcher in Game 2, a 4–1 Yankee loss. Johnny Podres and Ron Perranoski had a shutout going until Elston produced an RBI single in the ninth, his second hit of the day.

We went to Los Angeles for Game 3. It was the first time I'd been there, and I saw all these movie stars at the ballpark. Frank Sinatra and Doris Day were there. It felt like we were in a movie, a bad one. The Yankees lost Game 3 1–0. Don Drysdale pitched a three-hitter and fanned Elston twice. By Sunday night, after Koufax had beaten the Yankees 2–1 in Game 4, it was all over and we were headed home. That was the game Pepitone made that error when he failed to catch a throw to first base. "Elston was one of the first guys to come up to me in the dugout," Pepitone recalls. "He told me not to worry about it. It happens." Elston had two hits in the finale and finished the Series as the Yankees' leading hitter at .333. Unfortunately, the rest of the team did little else; the Yankees hit just .171 and scored only four runs.

Like everyone in New York, Elston was embarrassed and angry. "Sure, you can lose any World Series, but not lose in four games," he told the *Sporting News*. "I didn't dream that could happen. We weren't routed. We didn't collapse. We simply fell into a batting slump and ran into great pitching. But in those last three games we got great pitching, too."

Each of the Yankees got the loser's share of eight thousand dollars, while the Dodgers each pocketed twelve thousand dollars. After the Series, we went back to Teaneck and began preparing to move into our new house. The move coincided with the announcement of the Most Valuable Player award. The anxiety just about drove Elston crazy. He had two speaking dates—one in Utica; the other in Syracuse, each for five hundred dollars—and he canceled both engagements because he was too nervous. "If I win it I've got to be here," he told me. "I can't be somewhere else." Elston couldn't sleep, he didn't eat, and he couldn't sit still. For nearly two weeks, he'd toss and turn and wake up at five in the morning. Everywhere we'd go, people would come up to him and say, "Don't worry, you'll get it."

Finally, the news came on November 6. Elston's name was on every ballot. He received 248 points in balloting by the Baseball Writers Association. He got fifteen first-place votes out of twenty. Al Kaline of Detroit was second with 148 points. Whitey Ford was third.

"Elston would have won three or four MVPs had he not played behind Yogi," Clete Boyer said. "He was that good."

It was the eighteenth time a Yankee had won the MVP prize since Babe Ruth first won it in 1923. Winning the award meant so much to Elston. His name could be mentioned in the same breath as Ruth, Gehrig, DiMaggio, Rizzuto, Berra, Mantle, Maris. He was rightfully proud to be the first black man to win the Judge Kenesaw Mountain Landis Award in the American League. To Elston, the award also meant he could demand more money come contract time, and perhaps it could help him some day to become a major-league manager.

It was a wonderful day, and I remember it well because we were all but moved into the new house. Sportswriters and TV cameras were all over the place. For a while it seemed as though we were moving into a zoo. Elston Jr., who had just turned eight, did not understand what all the commotion was about. I told him it was like his father had won the Pulitzer Prize for baseball. That was the analogy I used.

One of the wire-service photographers asked Elston to pose for a picture, a photograph that ran the next day in just about every newspaper in the country. The photograph showed Elston with our three-year-old daughter Karen on his shoulders and big smiles on their faces. After posing for the shot, Elston carried her from room to room, all over the house, laughing all the way.

CHAPTER THIRTEEN

Elston Howard Night

*No catcher had an arm like Elston's. Not Yogi, not even Munson.
Elston had a rifle.*

—PHIL LINZ

IT DIDN'T TAKE LONG FOR THE HATE MAIL TO SHOW UP. AFTER ELSTON
won the MVP award, he got all kinds of letters. One day he showed
me one from somebody who had seen a picture of the two of us and
thought that Elston had married a white woman. The letter said, "Why
don't you stick to your own kind?" and things like that. I had to write
back and give a history lesson on why many black people like myself
have light complexions.

Elston always got lots of fan mail, and he tried to answer every letter,
even though there were dozens every day. After he got the MVP award,
it became too much for him to handle and he had to let the people at the
stadium take care of it. He also had to buy a lot of pictures because that's
what people wanted most. Elston even kept some in the glove compartment of his car. We also kept a stack by the front door of our new house.
Elston never seemed to mind when people would drive past our house,
stop, and come up to ring the doorbell and ask for autographed photos.

We loved our new house and enjoyed having our friends over for
dinner parties. I never got used to him being on the road all the time,
so when he was home we tried to make the most of it. Elston loved
to entertain, and we really took great pride in showing the house off.

Elston loved having friends around. Our parties became legendary. On any given night, our dining-room guests would include Carmen and Yogi Berra, Joan and Whitey Ford, Howard Cosell, Count Basie, Ed Sullivan, Jerry Vale, or even Allen and Rossi. One funny moment was the time George Crowe got upset at his wife, Yvonne, because she kept playing the same Sam Cooke record over and over again. George got so angry that he went to the record player, grabbed the record off the turntable, and smashed it into pieces.

I did most of the cooking for our parties, but Elston liked to cook, too. In fact, he cooked like a champion. He learned so many things from his days on the road. He learned how to cook Chinese food when he played in Toronto. He also could do crabs, chicken and gravy, or seafood with spaghetti. He knew how to make St. Louis spaghetti, which is different from regular spaghetti in that you cook it with the sauce and everything else thrown into it. I thought it was the strangest thing when I came to New York and saw how people cooked their spaghetti, then put their sauce on it. Elston knew how to cook rabbits and talked about how he used to catch them as a kid. Our children preferred plain food such as hamburgers and fries, but Elston and I considered ourselves to be gourmets. Much of our taste in food was developed during our extensive travels, particularly in Europe and Africa. Wherever we ate out, I found I could usually copy the dishes when I got home. Sometimes I would make beef Wellington with madeira sauce, usually served with vegetables I grew myself from our backyard. My other favorites were chicken Kiev and lobster thermador with Italian spinach. Elston had a wine cellar put in, which we stocked with dozens of bottles from around the world. For dessert we would have parfaits, or cakes, and everyone would leave by eleven o'clock quite satisfied.

Another good thing about our home was that we got to decorate it with exotic art from all over the world. Elston became an art fanatic like myself, so much so that there was hardly a vacant space on any of our walls. Much of our collection is the work of black artists whom we discovered on our travels to the Caribbean. Years later, we opened an art gallery.

The MVP award allowed us greater commercial opportunities. I am proud to say we were one of the first black families to be featured in

TV ads. In 1964, we did an oatmeal commercial with Whitey Ford and his family. An agency signed us to do a spot for H & O Oatmeal. They fixed up the studio to look like the Fords' kitchen. There were ten of us at the table, and everything was going well until the kids refused to eat the oatmeal. Whitey's son Ed was the toughest to convince. They put bananas on it, sugar, strawberries, anything just to get the kids to eat it. It was so funny.

Another big commercial deal came from Gulden's Mustard. This time I got to be the star. The commercial began with our kids coming into our kitchen, and I actually got to say to the camera, "Wonder why the hot dogs at Yankee Stadium are so good?" Years later, people still ask me about Gulden's Mustard. I also appeared on a billboard for Ballantine Beer. Elston, of course, had his own endorsement deals. His favorite came when he was asked to model for Cardinal Clothes in the April 1964 issue of *Gentleman's Quarterly*. The *New York Herald Tribune* said it may have been the first time a black man ever modeled clothing in a national magazine. That deal came about because Elston had become good friends with Bernie Miller, the publisher of *GQ*, who we met one weekend when we took the family to the Grossinger's resort in the Catskills. Bernie and his wife, Fran, became two of our closest friends and regularly attended our dinner parties and sat with me in the stands at Yankee home games.

Over the winter, Elston got to be a big man on the dinner circuit. He attended so many dinners that he got a little chubby, weighing as much as 210 pounds, about 10 pounds over his playing weight, before leaving for spring training. At one dinner in New York someone asked him if baseball would ever have a black manager. "I think so," he replied, "and relatively soon. Roy Campanella could have managed if he had not been hurt. Jackie Robinson could get a manager's job if he wanted it." Asked if he was interested, Elston replied, "I wouldn't hesitate. Baseball is my business."

Del Webb, owner of the Yankees, made Elston a very interesting offer. Webb made most of his money building homes in California and Arizona. In 1964 affirmative action was beginning to enter the public consciousness, and he probably thought it might be a good idea to hire a black executive. He told Elston he would build him a home out west and pay him lots of money if he would quit baseball and come work for him. Thirty-five years old and at the peak of his career, Elston turned him down. Little did we know that Webb and Dan Topping, the other Yankee owner, were about to sell the team to CBS.

Before he went to spring training, Elston got his new contract, which included a $10,500 raise. He was now making $60,000. Mickey Mantle had become baseball's highest-paid player when the Yankees gave him a $107,000 contract. Ralph Houk became the Yankee general manager in 1964, and Yogi replaced him as field manager, a move endorsed by Elston. "Everybody thinks Yogi's a funny fellow, but he can put his foot down. Don't forget there are plenty of older fellows around to keep young players in line. That's the Yankee way."

Not all the press about Elston was good. I always got angry when I read some of the things that were written about him in the black press. Elston was never outspoken on civil rights as Jackie Robinson was in later years, but that didn't mean he didn't care. It just was not in his personality to be too vocal, and I think that was true of a lot of the black ballplayers at that time. I wrote that writer a letter and chewed him out. He later apologized. A white writer asked Elston how he felt about the criticism. "Who am I to worry? It doesn't bother me neither what a man says as long as he doesn't hit me. But I ain't no Uncle Tom." When some athletes such as Muhammad Ali spoke out a few years later against the Vietnam War, Elston remained silent. Elston admired Ali as a boxer, but he believed sincerely that Ali should have served his country and accepted induction into the armed forces. Elston was an army veteran himself, and that's just the way he thought.

Yes, we were involved in the fight for civil rights, but we never bragged about it. We had other interests, too. Over the years we became very involved around Teaneck. Elston strongly believed in education, and he became an unpaid member on the school board and attended meetings whenever he could. He took part in "Plans for Progress," a program to encourage teenagers to stay in school. We were involved in the Teaneck High School PTA, and every year Elston would recruit some of his teammates to play in charity basketball games against the faculty. Fairleigh Dickinson University was aware of his local contributions and, in 1964, instituted a scholarship program in his name. We were happy to hear that George Crowe's daughter was the first recipient.

Elston got his MVP trophy on opening day at Yankee Stadium. Because opening day was delayed two days by rain, there was only a crowd of 12,709 on hand when Elston accepted the award from American League president Joe Cronin. Elston knew all about Judge Landis, the man for whom the trophy was named, and all the things he had done to keep blacks out of baseball, so he thought it was ironic and kind of funny that he would be the first black American Leaguer to win an award named for a racist baseball commissioner.

"It's a big thrill winning the MVP award," Elston told the media after he went 2-for-5 in the game, a 4–3 loss to Boston. "What I want now is that silver bat they give out for winning the batting title." Only two catchers had ever won batting titles, and the batting title was what he really wanted. Elston had come close twice, in 1958 and 1961. Asked how good his chances were, Elston said, "As good as anybody. Anybody with that kind of ambition has to work on it. It takes planning. That year I hit .348, I swung different than I ever had done before or since. That year I was a base-hit swinger, not a home-run swinger.

"The last three years I was more home-run conscious than ever before. When a big swinger gets that way, he naturally swings harder whether he realizes it or not. He also has a tendency to pull everything. That means those outside pitches with something on them result in pop-ups or ordinary flies to the outfield. What I've been doing this season is just the opposite. I am going with the pitch. If it's outside, I am hitting to right field, and I'm not taking my eyes off the pitch by swinging too hard. That's where the planning comes in. Once you get bit by the home-run bug, it's hard to shake the urge to go up there swinging from your heels on every pitch. In fact, I remember in '61 when I had that big batting average year. I hit quite a few home runs to the opposite field. Just swinging easy. I am convinced that the easy swing is the first thing a batter must do to get his batting average up there where it's respectable."

Asked if he considered 1963, his MVP season when he hit .287, his best year, he replied, "Why should I? Especially after the .348 I hit in 1961. If I did it once, I can do it again."

The Yankees were struggling along in fifth place in early June, but Elston was hitting the ball hard. In the first sixty-one games, he had driven in the deciding run seven times. On June 7 at Dodger Stadium against the Angels and pitcher Ken McBride, Elston hit a monster home run over the center-field wall. The media called it a "Frank Howard–like" shot; it helped give the Yankees a 9–3 victory. The Yankees went to Chicago on June 19 and, thanks to Elston, swept all four games. In the second game, Elston caught eleven innings and singled home the only run in a 1–0 win for Whitey Ford. In the Sunday doubleheader he homered, his sixth of the season, in the second inning of a 2–0 win. In the nightcap, Elston caught all seventeen innings and drove in the first run in a 2–1 win. On June 22, he sat out a 6–5 win, the Yankees' tenth straight. Later that day it was announced that he had been named as a starter for the All-Star Game at the new ballpark in Queens, Shea Stadium. "He is terrific in everything he does," said Chicago manager Al Lopez, who managed the American League squad that year. "Has real good power, can hit to all fields and is one of the best defensive catchers in the last twenty years. Very good for any club because he asserts himself the way a catcher should and takes charge."

Just before the All-Star Game, Double-Bubble Gum had an ad campaign in which they named Elston and Milwaukee catcher Joe Torre as their major-league catchers of the month. At the All-Star break Elston was hitting .292 with seven homers and 39 RBIs. Elston played all nine innings of the All-Star Game, and he was behind the plate when the National League's Johnny Callison hit a game-winning, three-run homer in the ninth inning off Dick Radatz.

In 1964 the Yankees were winning, but so were Baltimore and Chicago. "We're playing in a better league than the one we played last season, no question about it," Elston said. Things looked bleak when the Yankees went to Chicago in late August and lost four straight games to the White Sox. On that trip, Yogi got mad at Phil Linz because he was playing the harmonica on the team bus. Oh God! What a mess! That was a big incident. By August 22, the Yankees had lost six straight games. They were in Boston when Elston righted the ship with a three-run homer off Bill Monbouquette in the first game of a doubleheader. The Yankees won that one 5–3 and took the second game 8–0 behind rookie Mel Stottlemyre to get back into the race. Suddenly the Yankees were ready to make their pennant drive. Their starting pitching got a big boost when they brought up Stottlemyre from the minors. "This kid is one darn good pitcher," Elston said after the game in Boston.

One week later, on August 29 between games of a doubleheader with Boston, the Yankees held Elston Howard Night. In the first game, Elston went 1-for-3 as the Yankees won 10–2. Then came the big event. It was such a special night. It began with the Fairleigh Dickinson University marching band, dressed in kilts, parading on the field with drums and bugles. Near home plate all the dignitaries gathered around Mel Allen, the master of ceremonies. Elston remained back in the dugout, pacing nervously back and forth. Frank Crosetti, the veteran third-base coach, tried to calm him down. "Frank," Elston said, "this is the toughest thing in my life." Then John Blanchard led a parade of Yankees from the locker room onto the field. "All right, let's get Ellie out there on the field," yelled Joe Pepitone. "This is his show."

Mel Allen introduced all the guests. I stood near the mike with the kids and Elston's mother. Emmaline had come from St. Louis just for this night, and she received a warm reception from the Yankee Stadium crowd of 37,362. Finally, it was time for Elston, and he ran onto the field and was given a three-minute ovation. He waved repeatedly to the crowd and doffed his cap. I gave him a big hug and a kiss. Then came the gifts and all the tributes. First, there was a brand-new Chrysler Newport, then a piano. The players gave him a stereo player. Moose Skowron wasn't there, but he sent a silver service dining-room set. Bernie Miller, who helped organize the whole thing with our attorney Leonard Stone, presented Elston with a new wardrobe. John Drebinger of the *New York Times*, representing the New York Baseball Writers, presented him with a typewriter. "Someday, you'll join us in the press box and write your memoirs," he told Elston. Clete Boyer took the mike and saluted Elston for "his many years of great baseball." Mickey Mantle spoke. "Elston's one of the leaders of this club. His determination and attitude wears off on other players and makes the Yankees a team."

Finally, it was Elston's turn to speak. He didn't have much to say; he was too overcome by all the love. "I don't know where to begin," he said. "I'm very fortunate to be with the New York Yankees." The crowd cheered. Elston gave thanks to Bill Dickey, Ralph Houk, Yogi Berra, and his teammates. "This is the greatest thing in my life and I want to thank each and every one of you for making it possible."

Wrote Loften Mitchell in the *Amsterdam News*, "This was Elston Howard, eloquent but not loquacious, gentle but strong. This is a man whose acts and whose very character is represented in actions and deeds rather than words."

There were tears in Elston's eyes that night. More than ever, he was proud to be a Yankee.

Chapter Fourteen

The Elbow

*It's going to be a tough job finding kids to follow the likes of Dickey,
Berra and Howard.*
—Til Ferdenzi, *Sporting News*, 1965

Without Elston, the Yankees would not have won the pennant
in 1964. When September started, the team was in third place behind
Baltimore and Chicago. As the Yankees went 22–6 over the final month,
Elston kept coming up with big hits. On September 4, his homer helped
the Yankees beat Kansas City 9–7. On September 8 he drove in Mickey
Mantle with the winning run in a 2–1 victory over Minnesota. On September 10, his first-inning, three-run homer off Hank Aguirre led the
Yankees to a 5–2 win at Detroit. Two days later, he homered off Camilo
Pascual in the sixth inning of a 4–3 win over the Twins. On September 16
he went 3-for-4 and drove in two runs in a 9–4 win over the Angels. On
September 18 he went 2-for-4 and caught Whitey Ford's eighth shutout
of the season. The next day he went 2-for-5 with two RBIs in an 8–3 win
at Kansas City. The following day he went 1-for-3 and had an RBI in a
4–0 win over the Athletics. On September 22, Elston went 2-for-5 in a
5–3 win over Cleveland. On September 24 he homered off Luis Tiant in
a 4–3 win over the Indians as the Yanks won their ninth straight and took
a four-game lead over Baltimore. "Elston did all right for me," manager
Yogi Berra said. "He played hard and we won the pennant."

It didn't come easily. The Yankees clinched their twenty-ninth pennant on the next-to-last day of the season when Elston had two hits and drove in two runs in an 8–3 win over Cleveland. The Yankees finished with a 99–63 record, one game better than Chicago and two games better than Baltimore. Elston had a .313 batting average, 15 home runs, and 83 RBIs. He caught a career-high 147 games. He even had a stolen base and won the Gold Glove for the second straight season.

"I never felt like I had it made," Elston said in the September 12 issue of the *Sporting News*, in which he was pictured on the cover. "I always try to play like I haven't got there yet. It's been one long battle for me. As I look back over the years I can see where I've earned whatever I got. Nobody walked up to me and gave me anything. I think any kid starting out who thinks this is nuts. He's never going to make it any way. This baseball is a tough business. I mean by that you've got to have something to sell the owners. If you don't they are not going to dig in their pockets and pay you anything. You can't blame them. If you've got nothing to offer, they're not going to make it worth your while. You've got to like this game and you've got to take pride in the way you play it."

When it came time to play in his ninth World Series, Elston was glad to see that the St. Louis Cardinals had come from six games back in the final ten games and beat the Phillies for the National League pennant. For the first time, he would get to play in front of his hometown, in Sportsman's Park. He thought back to those days in 1947 when Teannie Edwards had taken him there to try out for the Cardinals, how well he had hit the ball, only to be passed over because he was black. Now he was coming home and playing in the World Series in front of his friends and family. When it comes World Series time, everybody is calling you up for tickets. Even the mailman. Even Elston's father, Travis. But Elston still had some issues with Travis, and he didn't return any of his phone calls when we got to St. Louis.

Elston had a good World Series, hitting .292, but the Yankees lost to the Cardinals in seven games. After going 2-for-5 in Game 1, a 9–5 loss, Elston went 1-for-4 with a double as the Yankees beat Bob Gibson 8–3 to even the Series. Back in New York for Game 3, Elston singled and scored in the second inning on Clete Boyer's double. In the ninth inning, with the game tied, Mickey Mantle came over to Elston in the on-deck circle as relief pitcher Barney Schultz warmed up and promised he would hit one out. Mickey did just that, and the Yankees won 2–1. The next day, in Game 4, Elston delivered an RBI single off Roger Craig as the Yankees scored three times in the first inning. Al Downing was pitching that day but he got into trouble in the sixth inning and had the bases loaded when he faced Ken Boyer. Elston called for a fastball. Al shook him off and decided to throw a changeup. Boyer didn't hit it real hard, but the ball reached the first row of seats in the left-field corner. The Cardinals won that game, 4–3.

The Yankees also lost Game 5 as Elston went hitless against Gibson. In the tenth inning, Bill White was on second base and Boyer was on first. Dick Groat tried to bunt, but he missed the pitch. With White leaning toward third, Elston came up firing and threw a strike to Phil Linz covering the bag at second. White knew he was trapped and, to his credit, immediately took off for third base. Linz's throw was off, and White made it to third base. A few pitches later Tim McCarver hit the decisive three-run homer.

Game 6 in St. Louis went to the Yankees, but the Cardinals won Game 7. Bob Gibson struck Elston out twice that day. When asked what it was like facing Gibson, Elston said, "He was quick, but I could see the ball. I just couldn't hit it." Naturally, Elston was sad. Nine times his Yankees had played in the World Series, and five times they had lost. Four times they were beaten in the seventh game.

Still, Elston had enjoyed another productive season. He was at the peak of his playing career. Over a ten-year period he had made only twenty-eight errors as a catcher. His fielding percentage was nearly impeccable. So when the Yankees sent his contract for the 1965 season, I thought it was an insult. They offered him the same salary of sixty thousand dollars that he had made in 1964. The agent in me got quite upset, and I told Elston to turn it down. For all those years that the Yankees held him back, I still to this day believe he deserved better contracts. He deserved to be paid more for all those years he played in the outfield and sat on the bench waiting for Yogi Berra to retire. Catchers like Elston had limited career spans. What about Elston? There was no free agency. The Yankees had no right to deny him the right to make a better salary.

I'll never forget those nights when Elston would come home angry and upset in the early days when the Yankees were holding him back. It was me who felt the brunt. I had to be wife, mother, and psychiatrist sometimes. In 1964 he was the most productive player on a team that had won five straight pennants. There was no doubt in my mind that he deserved more money. Honestly, it was horrible how ballplayers were treated in those days. When the Yankees upped their offer to seventy thousand, I told Elston, "No, they can do better." But Elston never liked to make waves. We talked about it, but I eventually gave in and our "marital crisis" was over. Elston signed, and the press called him the highest-paid catcher in baseball. How pitiful! He deserved more money.

Casey Stengel knew how valuable Elston was. When *New York Post* columnist Jimmy Cannon asked the Mets manager what he thought of Elston's 1965 contract, he said, "Whatever they're paying him, it ain't enough." Casey was dead right.

On February 18, the Yankees called a press conference for Elston. A photographer shoved two heads of soggy lettuce into his hands to symbolize the "green" he was getting. Elston said he expected to be around another five years as a player. Then he raised a few eyebrows when he said his long-range goal was to be major-league baseball's "first Negro manager."

The Yankees meanwhile had a new manager; they had fired Yogi. When a newspaper writer asked Elston about it, Elston said it was because Yogi was not communicating with all the players. Personally, he hated to see Yogi go. Furthermore, the Yankees hired Johnny Keane from the Cardinals to replace Yogi. Elston was mystified.

Elston had hit .313 in 1964 and vowed he would leave the home-run hitting to Maris and Mantle. When he headed for spring training in February 1965, he again was determined to win a batting title, the one that he never got to win in 1958 or 1961. The Yankees never played well in spring training, but this year there were a bunch of trouble signs. Whitey Ford's spring-training ERA was 6.09, and he had circulatory problems in his arm. Joe Pepitone hurt his left hand after getting hit by a Jim Kaat pitch. He hit .067 in the spring.

The real decisive blow came on April 3 when the Yankees played the Pittsburgh Pirates in an exhibition game on a wet field in San Juan,

Puerto Rico. Elston was catching Al Downing that day, and his foot slipped as he tried to make a pickoff throw. He hurt his elbow and didn't catch any more games that exhibition season. When the Yankees went to Houston for an exhibition series on April 9 to christen the Astrodome, Elston could only pinch-hit. Still, the worst thing he did was deciding that he had to play on opening day. The Yankees were in Minnesota, and Johnny Keane was eager to start the season with his best lineup. The weather was not good. The day before it had rained all day and the temperatures never made it over 35 degrees. Still, Keane asked Elston to play. "Heck, you know I was gonna try," Elston said later. "That was a big mistake," Al Downing would later recall. "Elston had no business playing that day."

Elston did fine at the plate; he homered and doubled off the wall. He caught all eleven innings that day, but his elbow really began to hurt.

Funny thing, as cold and miserable as opening day was, the next day was sunny and a lot warmer, but it was an off day. It would have been a lot better had the Twins postponed the game.

"[The elbow] was all right for a while that afternoon," Elston told *Newsday*'s Joe Donnelly. "But the Twins were doing a lot of running. They made me keep throwing and by the end of the day I was back where I had been a week before."

The next day Elston couldn't bend his arm to eat breakfast. His elbow was noticeably swollen. He tried to catch again that Sunday, but the pain only got worse. He threw a ball away and a run scored. "I started to take off my glove," he said. "I wanted to throw it into the stands. I hate making errors."

Elston admitted that playing on opening day was a mistake. "I can't play," he said on April 13. "I can't throw. I could not throw hard in the eleventh inning on Monday. Now I can't even straighten out my arm. I shouldn't have played Monday. Now it looks like I'll miss another week."

For treatment, the Yankees sent Elston to Los Angeles to see Dr. Robert K. Kernlan, a famous orthopedic surgeon who was treating Sandy Koufax's left arm. As Elston walked into the office, he saw Elgin Baylor, the Los Angeles Lakers basketball star, limp away on sore knees. "I'm sure glad that I'm not as bad off as that poor guy," Elston said.

Dr. Kernlan said Elston's problem was an inflammation of the throwing elbow. He said there are only so many throws in a catcher's arm, and that maybe Elston had used them all up. "He told me I should rest it," Elston told the media. "Because the next time I play when I'm not ready it could be the last time."

Dr. Sidney Gaynor, the club physician, took charge of Elston's treatments, and eventually it was his decision to operate. After a game in Kansas City, Elston didn't catch another game until June 13. John Blanchard and Bob Schmidt platooned while Elston rested up and did some pinch-hitting. Elston's fan mail was up. One fan sent him a religious medal that he kept in his pants pocket. Some fans sent letters prescribing miracle ointments for his arm.

Just as Elston was recovering, I found out that I was a diabetic. While working in the garden one day, I became very thirsty and dizzy. I didn't know the symptoms of diabetes, but I should have because I knew my father was a diabetic. I think Elston being hurt, taking the kids to school, and caring for Karen brought it all on. I felt so sick, and I had lost some weight, so I called our doctor, Dr. John Lathen, over in Hackensack. He told me to come right over. He examined me and took a blood test, then told me to go to the hospital immediately. At first, I was in denial about my condition, but once you realize you have it, you have to learn to live with it. I had to take insulin shots and change my diet. No ice cream, no candy. I began seeing a specialist; I had no idea he was the same doctor who was treating Jackie Robinson. Jackie was very discreet about his diabetes. Nobody knew about it, but the doctor told me. He said Jackie was not a very good patient. A few weeks later we went to a party hosted by Marian Logan, and Jackie was there. Around that time Jackie had had a slight stroke—you could see it in his face—but that was kept quiet. I told Jackie that I, too, was a diabetic, and we had a good talk about it. I asked him if he was taking his insulin and eating right and he admitted he wasn't. I could never understand why he didn't. His wife, Rachel, was a nurse. He could have taken better care of himself.

With Elston hurting, the Yankees began to fade in the standings. John Blanchard was not a good thrower and a lot of teams were running on him. On May 3, the Yankees made a trade, sending Blanchard and pitcher Rollie Sheldon to Kansas City for a good-glove, no-hit catcher named Doc Edwards. Elston's locker was right next to Blanchard's, and he never forgot the scene in the clubhouse that day: Blanchard sitting on his stool in his undershorts and Yankee shirt, crying like a baby.

"God, good God," Elston recalled at the time. "It makes you sick." Fighting back the tears, Blanchard took off his uniform for the last time and put it in his bag. "I'll take this with me," he said. "Maybe some day I'll come back." With the acquisition of Edwards, Elston was told the very next day to check into Lennox Hill Hospital for bone-chip surgery. Elston was told he would miss six weeks.

"They cut a chip out of Elston's elbow, but they cut Blanchard's heart out," wrote Maury Allen in the *Post*. Elston left the hospital a few days later with the bone chips in a small glass case. He joked he would put them on display with his MVP plaque and two Gold Gloves. But as soon as he got home, he threw them in the garbage. Sitting around waiting to heal drove Elston crazy. It was hard to keep his mind off baseball, particularly with the Yankees struggling in the standings. On June 1, Elston still couldn't throw, but he could swing the bat. So he told Keane he was available for pinch-hitting duty.

In his first at-bat since April 28, Elston came up with the bases loaded in the thirteenth inning of a game against the White Sox. He hit a long foul ball to left field off knuckleballer Eddie Fisher before striking out. Elston got his revenge the next day when he delivered a pinch-hit single off Fisher with the bases loaded in the tenth inning to give the Yankees a 4–3 win.

Elston's return was a shot in the arm for the Yankees' fading pennant hopes. They won nine of thirteen, but they were 9½ games behind Minnesota. And there were other problems. Mantle had bad legs. Roger Maris had hamstring problems. Tony Kubek had shoulder trouble. Bobby Richardson was bothered by a leg bruise. Jim Bouton and Whitey Ford were losing games. Ford, too, was having arm problems, and he tried to help Elston. There was some stuff called DMSO, which they use on horses when their legs get sore, and Whitey tried rubbing some on Elston's elbow. "Hey, that's not bad," Elston told Whitey. Elston went out that day and threw the ball around pretty well. But the relief was temporary.

Elston's arm never really got much better. He played in 110 games, most of them as a pinch-hitter. His .233 batting average was his lowest in eleven seasons in New York. All of a sudden, the Yankees were an old team, and they finished in sixth place with a 77–85 record. It had become evident that age had caught up with the Yankees. The team was relying on no-name players such as Steve Whitaker and Roger Repoz. Unfortunately, the Yankees were now paying the price for all those years when George Weiss chose not to sign black players. The farm system was all but bare, except for a nineteen-year-old shortstop from Oklahoma named Bobby Murcer.

"I always considered Elston as being one of the friendliest, kindest people I ever met in baseball," Bobby recalls. "When I first arrived on the scene in 1966, I was very young, very green, even though I had made the team as a shortstop. Johnny Keane was the manager and Vern Benson was his right-hand man, his number-one coach. One day standing around the batting cage Elston overheard Vern telling me that he couldn't believe how such a young man like me could have such bad hands and be a shortstop. Well, Ellie didn't know me that well, but he took offense. He tapped Benson on the shoulder and as Benson turned, he said, 'Let me say this to you, Mr. Benson: If I ever hear you say that again to this young man, I'll personally kick your ass.' On that Yankee ball club for him to stick up for me to a coach, I gained immediate respect for Elston. Ellie had a friend for life."

In the spring of 1966, Elston began swimming daily at the Jewish Center around the corner, hoping his elbow injury was behind him. He was full of confidence. "My arm is completely healed and I don't expect any trouble at all," he declared. "I'm in very good shape now. It won't take me long to get ready in spring training and I am confident I will have a good year. I will play as many games as Johnny Keane wants me to and I will catch doubleheaders if the man says so."

Ralph Houk, still the Yankee general manager, felt Elston would make it back, so much so that he traded Doc Edwards. Kubek, just twenty-nine, announced his retirement, and to fill the void at shortstop, Houk traded Phil Linz to the Phillies for Ruben Amaro. The Yankees also were hoping Murcer would be the next Mickey Mantle and make everybody forget about how old the team really was.

The Yankees did have some promising players. That spring, Elston liked a rookie left-hander named Fritz Peterson. "The kid pitches just like Whitey. He's got a fastball that moves, a high-class breaking ball and most important of all, he can get the breaking ball over the plate when he's behind in the count. Believe me, you won't find many left-handers who can do that—just like Whitey."

Fritz always appreciated Elston's kindness. "He was a very nice guy to young people," he recalls. "He was a lot of fun, with a good sense of humor. Coming onto a team with the big names, you had guys like the Hal Reniffs who laughed at you. But Elston was always real nice to me, like Mantle. Elston was good to pitch to. He made you feel like a pitcher out there, not a stranger."

The Yankees got off to a wretched start, and before April was over Keane had been fired and Murcer was sent to the minors. Elston had taken a liking to Keane. He was a decent man, but he was no Ralph Houk. So Elston was happy when "The Major" gave up his job as general manager and returned to the dugout. The cold weather was no help to Elston's elbow, which once again started swelling. By May 16, he had thrown out only two of fourteen base stealers, and he had made five throwing errors. Once again, he would come home moody, in his own world. Sometimes he wouldn't speak to me or the children. "My arm isn't right," he said one cold day in Detroit. "It is sore. It hurts here in the elbow. It hasn't been right ever since the operation and I can't straighten it out.

"It can't be bone chips this time. There is no swelling. Last year my elbow puffed up. All I know is that it hurts. I have never thrown so erratically. Sometimes I get zip on the ball and sometimes the throws are weak and wide, high or low. Even when Aparicio was going good, he didn't run on me. Nobody ran on me."

Yankee pitchers took notice of Elston's problem and began to hurry their deliveries to the plate. Said Houk, "I think we'll have to wait for warmer weather to see if his arm is as bad as it looks now. It could be the cold that we have had to play in every game that has caused his elbow to get sore." Elston's arm woes also brought about a slump at the plate. He began to try for more home runs. His average suffered, too, falling as low as .157. Houk never wavered in his support. "You're going to be in there even if you have to kick it down to second base," he told Elston.

On May 17, Elston laughed off media talk, notably from Dick Young in the *Daily News*, that he was finished. "If it's all over," he told the press, "I'll call a big press conference in my house and we'll have a party." But things didn't get better. In Cleveland, Max Alvis took a big swing and the backlash of the bat caught Elston in the head. Two days later Elston became one of the first catchers to wear the cut-down protective batting helmet behind the plate. "I know I'm going to wear this for a while," Elston said. "That headache I got from Alvis's bat went away, and I don't want it to come back."

It was sometime around then that Elston renewed his faith in God. Elston was always a religious man, but I think his prayers now had a specific purpose. "I respected Elston tremendously as a player and a Christian," Bobby Richardson says. Together, Richardson and Elston were responsible for the formation of the Baseball Chapel, an organization that sets up services for major-league players who cannot attend regular Sunday services while on road trips. Protestant services were often held late in the morning, just as the players were leaving for the ballpark. In 1965 Elston and Bobby organized prayer meetings before Sunday games on the road. "Elston would help round up the players," Bobby recalls. "He would go up to them and say, 'I want you to be there.' By the final week of the season, we had the whole team there."

Years ago, after Elston's death, the late Red Barber wrote an article on how he became involved with the Yankee team services. He thought back to the day Elston and Bobby came to him for help. "I thought about it. The black player and the white player together earnestly searching for a Sunday church service far from home. I talked about it with Howard and with Richardson. It was a touchy subject. We decided to do something about it. We planned to have a meeting in the hotel at ten o'clock on road Sundays to last about fifteen minutes. Howard and Richardson challenged me to lead the meeting when they said, 'You're a lay reader, aren't you?'

"We went to manager Johnny Keane, who said it was all right with him, maybe a good thing provided nothing was said in the clubhouse and that no written notices were posted. Richardson and Howard went from player to player each road Sunday with the location of the hotel room. At the season's end, some thirty-two different Yankee players and coaches had attended."

By June 24, God began to answer some of Elston's prayers. Warm weather came, and Elston's batting average rose with the thermometer. He hit the only grand slam of his major-league career in a 5–2 victory over the White Sox. "See, they said the old man was through. I told you I'd be all right as soon as the warm weather came," said Elston, who was now hitting .275. "I'm not through. No, sir. I'll tell you when I'm through. I won't fool nobody, not old Elston Howard."

Elston didn't make the All-Star team in 1966. By August, it became apparent the Yankees and the rest of the American League were no match for Frank Robinson and the Baltimore Orioles. By September, the Yankees were rapidly heading south in the standings. They began bringing up more of their so-called prospects. Mel Stottlemyre, who had won twenty games in 1965, was now headed for 12–20 record. The Yankees had no bullpen stopper. They lost thirty-eight one-run games.

It was just an awful year for Elston. He played in only 126 games and hit .256 with just six homers and 35 RBIs. There was talk that Elston would be moved to first base in 1967 to make room for Jake Gibbs, who had hit .258 in sixty-two games. "I would love to play first base," Elston said. "I think I might last two or three more years as a first baseman." Unfortunately, Mickey Mantle's bad knees meant he could not play the outfield any more, so the Yankees began thinking of playing him at first base. Elston kept the faith.

"How could a club with a Mickey Mantle, Roger Maris, Tom Tresh, Clete Boyer, Joe Pepitone, Mel Stottlemyre, Fritz Peterson, Al Downing, and Fred Talbot finish in the cellar?" Elston said. "I can't figure it out."

The Yankees were the laughingstocks of baseball. Elston was not laughing.

CHAPTER FIFTEEN

The Impossible Dream

Trading him to Boston, we thought we were doing him a favor.
—RALPH HOUK

FOR THE 1967 SEASON, THE YANKEES WANTED ELSTON TO TAKE A ten-thousand-dollar pay cut. A pay cut! We could not afford one. We had three children and a mortgage. To me, this was totally unacceptable and, of course, I said so. There was no way that Elston should be penalized for being injured. Was it his fault that the New York Yankees were not the New York Yankees any more? Was it his fault they had finished in last place? Elston, too, was unhappy when he got the offer from the Yankee front office. The contract arrived shortly before we took the family on a two-week January vacation.

We rarely took the kids on our off-season vacations because they were in school, but Elston was determined to spend more time with his family. So we were all together when the bad news came. We were on a cruise, just off the coast of Aruba, when word came by phone that Elston's mother had suffered a stroke and died on January 21 in St. Louis. Elston was devastated. We had to get home immediately, but it took several days. We had to get back on the boat and go to Jamaica. When we got there, we had to wait for two more days because there were no everyday flights to New York. It was such a helpless feeling. And when we got back to New York, we had to leave straight for St. Louis. It was very draining for all of us. After the funeral, that's when Elston told me that if anything ever happened to him, to bury him the next day.

Following the funeral, Elston turned his attention back to baseball and his contract dispute. When the newswriters called him, Elston wasn't shy about voicing his displeasure at the Yankee offer. He declared himself healthy again. There was no more pain in his elbow, he said. All winter long he had worked out at a nearby gym and spent hours in the family basement swinging a bat. "I've been thinking about it all winter," he told the *New York Post*. "I'm switching to a lighter bat and going for the long ball. I think I can hit thirty or thirty-five homers. I feel I can hit home runs without too much damage to my average. Mainly, I want to help the ball club get moving again. I believe I can have a good year. I know I'm older, but I won't be going into the season hurting. Last year my arm wasn't right until June."

When it came time for pitchers and catchers to report for spring training in mid-February, I told Elston to stay home. Once again, he was holding out, and this time we were serious. "The club's always been good to me," Elston said. "I never had no trouble and I never been no problem to anybody. I don't know why this should be such a problem. My sweaters are still packed. I hope to be down [to Fort Lauderdale] some day this week."

The New York writers sided with Elston, and I think this helped give him some leverage with Lee McPhail, the Yankee general manager. "This Elston Howard business is too ridiculous," wrote Vic Ziegel in the *Post*. "Here's Howard, the all-time company man, getting the miseries from the team he has loved for so long."

Elston's "rebellion" ended after four days when he and McPhail agreed on a sixty-four-thousand-dollar contract. It was a six-thousand-dollar cut. I shook my head and let him sign it. "I lost the battle, but I'm still betting I'll win the war," Elston told the press. "I took the cut in salary with a clause that I can get it back with a good year.

"I always gave 100 percent. Now with this incentive I'll give 125 percent. I'm not what you call a real tough negotiator. You don't want no one hating you for a few dollars."

McPhail was not as diplomatic. He said he was only reacting to the reality of what was then modern-day baseball when he said, "Generally, the better young players are underpaid and the older ones overpaid."

The Yankee team that headed north for opening day was mostly a team of no-names, has-beens, and vagabonds. Bobby Richardson and Tony Kubek had retired. Roger Maris was traded to St. Louis for Charley Smith. Clete Boyer was traded to Atlanta. Jim Bouton was in the minors at Syracuse. Hal Reniff was with the Mets. Joe Pepitone was in center field so that Mickey Mantle could play first base. Even in the broadcasting booth there were changes. Red Barber had been fired.

On opening day in Washington, Elston homered in an 8–0 victory. Two days later, on April 14, came the Yankee home opener. It was a game Elston would never forget. We were playing the Red Sox; a young rookie left-hander named Bill Rohr was making his major-league debut for Boston. In the ninth inning, he was pitching a no-hitter. Tom Tresh led off the ninth with a hard shot to left field, but Carl Yastrzemski made an incredible somersault catch, and the Yankees were two outs away from the ultimate embarrassment. After Bobby Cox made out, up came Elston. Everybody knew what was at stake. The Yankee crowd was cheering for Rohr as he worked the count to 3 and 2, then threw Elston a hard curveball. Elston took a mighty cut at the pitch and slashed a hard, clean single to right field. If not for Elston's hit, Rohr would have been the first player to pitch a no-hitter in his first major-league start. When Elston got to first base, to his bewilderment, he was booed by the crowd of 14,375. Booed by Yankee fans who had cheered him for twelve years; booed for doing his job, like always. We had a big dinner party that night, and someone from one of the local newspapers showed up and took pictures. I can tell you Elston was not a very good host that night. He hardly said a word. The booing hurt him plenty.

"My job is to hit the ball and I've got three kids to feed and that's what I do," he told the press, almost apologetically. "When I got to first base, I looked at [Rohr]. I knew he was hurt. But that's my job, man."

Elston's pride was further hurt in the coming days when he began to receive hate mail. "That was not a very nice thing you did to Bill Rohr," one letter said. "I despise you for it." It was signed by "an ex-Yankee fan." Isn't that pathetic? Some of these people had no brains at all. Elston opened another letter. "Sorry," it said. "You stink in my book." And that was one of the nicer ones.

Elston took time out to write back to some of those folks who had been courageous enough to sign their names. "I got one letter from a young girl who didn't know a thing about baseball," he recalled. "She told me I shouldn't have stopped Rohr from becoming famous. I told her to write Rohr and tell him the next time he pitches he ought to lay the ball in for me four times so I can hit four home runs and have a chance to become famous, too.

"I've broken up no-hitters for better pitchers than that kid," Elston said. "I remember breaking up a no-hitter for Herb Score one night [in 1957], but nobody got mad. From the way some people write, they wanted me to lay down."

When the newspapers published stories about all the bad mail, Elston received a second batch of mail from "nice people" who appreciated Elston's professionalism.

"Dear Mr. Howard:

I saw the game where you broke up Rohr's no-hitter in the ninth inning and I say I'm glad. I read in the paper that some fans thought you should not have gotten a hit, but that's what you were there for. If Rohr really deserved to get a no-hitter, he would have struck you out, and my brother feels the same way." The letter was signed Jim Kapsales, *New York Post*, April 19, 1967.

Elston Jr. was eleven years old at the time and his Little League teammates teased him about it. When he came home he was troubled by some of the things he had heard. I told him, "Your father has to make a living like anyone else."

Elston soon gained a reputation for being "The Spoiler" that season. One week later in Boston, Elston had a two-run single in the eighth inning to end Rohr's bid to become the eighth rookie pitcher to break into the majors with back-to-back shutouts. One week later against the White Sox, Gary Peters retired the first twelve batters before Elston singled in the fifth.

Ever wonder what happened to Bill Rohr? After his two wins over the Yankees, he didn't win another game the rest of the season. The next year the Red Sox traded him to Cleveland and by the time he was twenty-two, he was finished in baseball. Nowadays, he is a lawyer specializing in medical malpractice, living in Palm Springs, California.

The Yankees started the 1967 season fairly well, but it soon became obvious they were headed for another second-division finish. Whitey Ford had a 2–4 record in late May when doctors told him he was going to need elbow surgery. Whitey decided to retire instead. Elston and Whitey were always very close. I know Whitey relied on Elston quite a bit at the end of his career. It was no secret that Elston would help him out every so often; sometimes he'd scratch up the ball, rub it in the mud, or wet it down. "We used to needle him about how he would scuff up the ball for Whitey," says Jim Kaat, the Minnesota Twins pitcher who came to know Elston in the late '70s when he was traded to the Yankees. "He would just laugh.

With the TV cameras they have today, they would have picked that right up. Back then from the dugout we could see him pick up a gob of mud or scuff the ball with his kneepads."

Kaat says he always dreaded pitching to Elston, even in 1967. "I would fear Elston more than I did Mickey," says Kaat, a left-hander. "In 1967, we lost the pennant by one game and toward the end of July there was a game where I had a 1–0 shutout going into the last inning. Mickey was at the plate, but I looked over at the on-deck circle and saw Elston and I said to myself, 'I'm not going to let Howard hit one into the right-center field seats.' My strength was pitching low and away and he covered the outside of the plate so well. So I gave up a game-tying home run to Mickey and we lost 3–1."

On June 26 Elston took a foul tip off the bat of Rick Monday that bent his finger way out of shape. Trainer Joe Soares pulled it back into place, but the next day it was discovered he had a bone chip in his ring finger. He was out of the Yankee lineup for about a week. When he returned on July 1, it was too soon. His batting average began to tumble, falling below .200. Ralph Houk began platooning him with Jake Gibbs. On August 2 during a game with the Angels I was sitting with our friend

Bernie Miller, and he told me there were rumors that Elston might be traded. In the ninth inning Elston came to the plate as a pinch-hitter for pitcher Joe Verbanic. He struck out; it would be his last at-bat as a Yankee. After the game, a reporter came up to him and asked if he indeed had been traded. Elston knew nothing about it, and said so.

The next morning the phone rang at 8:30. It was raining outside, and Ralph Houk was on the line. "I don't want to shock you," he said to Elston. Elston knew right away. "I must have been traded," he replied. Lee McPhail had made the deal the night before in Chicago: Elston was going to the Boston Red Sox for the twenty-thousand-dollar waiver price and two players to be named after the season was over. When Elston hung up the phone, he was visibly shaken, almost to the point of tears. I thought he was going to tell me that there was no way he would go to Boston. Years before he had been assured by management that he would always be a Yankee.

Houk said he was doing Elston a favor; the Red Sox were in the thick of the pennant race. Actually, the trade was a rotten thing to do. Imagine if the Yankees had traded Mickey Mantle. We had seen dozens of ballplayers come and go, families constantly uprooted. We never thought it would happen to us. We had been fortunate to be able to buy a home in Teaneck and stay. Under today's rules, Elston could have vetoed the trade: he would have been a ten-and-five man (ten years in the majors, five with the same club) with the power to reject a trade. A few years later players would have this right, after Curt Flood's successful challenge to Major League Baseball's reserve clause. Flood was a saint, but he was too late to help Elston in 1967.

Even though Elston was obviously upset, I was delighted. I loved Boston, and I saw they were in second place. The Yankees were not the Yankees we had known and loved. They had become a completely different organization. I could never get used to mediocrity, and that's what we had. Elston said he needed time to think it over.

If Elston had to be traded, I was glad it was to Boston. In Boston, he was only two hundred miles from home. We would get an apartment up there and bring the family up on weekends. Had he been traded to some team out west, I know he would not have gone. That afternoon Elston went to the stadium to clean out his locker. He thought it would take only thirty minutes, but he stayed for three hours to accommodate the late-arriving press. He met with Houk before the players started arriving for that night's game against the Angels. Most of the players didn't know about the deal until they arrived at the ballpark. Some of them seemed almost envious that Elston was being traded to a contender.

Joe Pepitone, always joking around, shook hands with Elston and said, "Get me traded." Elston laughed and replied, "You're doing a pretty good job of it yourself. You don't need help."

Phil Rizzuto walked in. "Holy cow! I almost drove off the bridge," he told Elston. "I heard it on the car radio." Phil knew the shock Elston was experiencing: he too had been sent packing eleven years earlier, when he was released by the Yankees. "I know how bad you feel, Ellie," Rizzuto said. "But you're much better off than I was. You're going to a contender, and they really want you. I was just dropped. When I was released I wanted to jump off the Brooklyn Bridge. Just think everything over very carefully after you get out of here. Remember, once you're out of baseball, they forget you right away. Look at Bobby Richardson—nobody even mentions him any more."

As each reporter asked the same questions over and over again, Elston found the smiles harder to come by. He told the reporters that he was still undecided about going to Boston. Maybe, just maybe, he would retire after all. "I don't know if I'm going to go or not," he kept repeating, as if he didn't believe his own words. "I would be happy to be with a contender, but after so many years with the same organization, I don't know about anyone else. Houk is the greatest manager I have ever played for, and Casey Stengel and Lee McPhail were always great to me."

Red Sox owner Tom Yawkey called. "We want you," he told Elston. Houk said he felt bad about trading Elston, but the decision was made to rebuild with youth. Mickey Mantle was the only "old-timer" left.

"It was as tough a thing as I've ever had to do," Houk said later. "When we got to the ballpark later, we had another long talk, I could see how bad he felt."

Elston thought of all the good games he had at Fenway Park, and the wall—the Green Monster—in left field. He thought back to his very first

major-league game with the Yankees in 1955. He had a talk with Bernie
Miller, who reminded him that with Boston he might be able to play in
his tenth World Series. Haywood Sullivan, Boston's general manager,
called. By six o'clock that night, Elston's mind was made up—he was
joining the Red Sox. He went to the phone and called Elston Jr., who was
away at summer camp. Elston wanted him to know. Karen, Cheryl, and
I could only watch as he packed his bags. We were in tears. We assured
him everything would be all right; we'd meet him in Boston. The next day
he flew out to join the Red Sox in Minnesota.

"Haywood Sullivan said he believed I could help the Red Sox, not
only for the rest of this season, but for a few more years to come, both
with my hitting, my catching, and ability to help their young pitchers,"
Elston told sportswriter Jim Ogle. "Baseball is in my blood. If I can help
the Red Sox win the pennant this year it would be the greatest thrill of
my career. "Mr. Yawkey told me he'd be proud to have me on his team.
Boston has a lot of good strong, young arms. They scored a lot of runs.
It's a real contender, and if I can help them as they tell me I can, I'll be
happy to do my best for them."

The next day, Carl Yastrzemski spoke for all of Boston when he said,
"I'm happy Elston Howard's coming. He calls a game better than anyone
I ever saw. I've always regarded Howard a good clutch hitter in the years
I played against him."

Not everyone was happy with Elston's trade. Some members of the
New York media were outraged, especially with the move coming so late
in the season after the trading deadline. In similar late-season trades Ken
Boyer and Rocky Colavito had gone to the White Sox. Leonard Koppett
of the *New York Times* wrote that the late-season deals were "dishonest"
and "disgraceful" and made a pitch to the American League commissioner William Eckert to step forward and stop deals like the one that
had sent Elston to Boston.

Wrote Koppett: "What's wrong with such deals? Two things: They
violate the perfectly clear intent of a long-standing rule that no major
trades should be made after June 15 to prevent a pennant contender
from bolstering himself down the stretch by picking off high-quality
players from non-contending teams. And they undermine the elaborate

structure of belief baseball has constructed to make sure that a man won't be playing today's game against tomorrow's employer and be aware of it."

Yankee fans, too, were up in arms. The fourteen-year-old son of Yankee president Michael Burke wrote his mother a letter from summer camp. "Mom, how could Dad ever trade Elston Howard to the Red Sox? It wasn't right, is it?"

Dick Williams, Boston's manager, who was two years younger than Elston, welcomed him to his new club. The clubhouse manager put number 18 on his uniform because one of the coaches, Eddie Kasko, was wearing 32. A Boston reporter asked Williams if Elston could play one hundred games for him. "That might be rather difficult," Williams replied, "since there's only sixty games left."

On August 4 in Minnesota, Elston spent his first game with the Red Sox on the bench. The next game was the NBC Saturday "Game of the Week." Elston came to bat with the bases loaded against Twins right-hander Dave Boswell. He struck out. Two weeks later, on August 18, Elston looked on in horror when Tony Conigliaro was beaned by Angels pitcher Jack Hamilton, fracturing his cheekbone. It brought to mind the time in 1957 when Herb Score was hit by a ball off the bat of Gil McDougald.

"It was the nastiest thing I've ever seen," said Reggie Smith, a twenty-two-year-old rookie outfielder on the Red Sox. "Elston told me about McDougald and the ball that hit Herb Score. We thought Tony was gonna die, especially when they called for a priest and last rites were given in the clubhouse. It was eerie. Nobody wanted to talk about it. Tony C. was lying there, his eye had popped out."

Elston said he had never seen an injury like Conigliaro's. His eye socket was crushed. Elston had immediate doubts that Tony would ever play again. Conigliaro did come back, but sadly, he never made it all the way back. If anything good came out of the ugly scene, it was that the Red Sox began to win more ball games.

Elston broke through on August 21. Using a borrowed bat from second baseman Mike Andrews, his ninth-inning single to left center with the bases loaded drove in Jerry Adair (another late Boston acquisition) with the winning run to beat the Senators 6–5. The victory, Boston's fifth straight, left the Red Sox right on the heels of the White Sox and Twins. Elston was hopeful about the team's chances. "It was a tough break losing Tony Conigliaro, but these guys are trying a little harder. Jim Lonborg is the best pitcher in the American League and one of the best I've caught, and I've caught a few good ones."

On August 28 Elston came home. More than twenty-seven thousand fans turned out to see his return to Yankee Stadium. Elston came back to Teaneck before the game and was nervous all afternoon. When he came to the plate that night, the same fans who earlier that season had booed him for breaking up a no-hitter erupted in cheers. Then came the familiar voice of PA announcer Bob Sheppard: "Now batting for the Red Sox, number 18, Elston Howard." I still love listening to Sheppard's voice. He's so good. Wrote Maury Allen in the *Post*, "Howard stood embarrassed with his bat in his hand, pumping it self-consciously back and forth as the sound rolled through the stadium."

"That was the best ovation I ever got in my life," Elston said later. Batting against Fred Talbot with two runners on, Elston grounded out to end the inning. In the fourth he flied to right field, and in the sixth he lined a single to center to score a run as the Yankee crowd cheered again. Reggie Smith homered in the eighth for the final Boston run and the Red Sox won 3–2. In the sixth, when the Yankees loaded the bases, Dick Williams brought in a young left-hander, Sparky Lyle, from the bullpen. When Lyle arrived, Elston told him to throw breaking balls. The batter was Steve Whitaker, whose Yankee locker had been right next to Elston's. Whitaker was called out looking on a wide-sweeping curve, then Charley Smith grounded out, and the Yankees were on their way to a ninth-place finish. Lyle knew better than to shake Elston off. Williams had warned all his pitchers that if any of them did, they would be fined fifty dollars.

One of the most memorable plays in Red Sox history occurred on August 29, the day before Thurgood Marshall was appointed to the U.S. Supreme Court. The Red Sox were a half-game up on Minnesota before the start of a doubleheader in Chicago. In the first game, Boston was leading 4–3, but the White Sox had Ken Berry at third base with one out. Duane Josephson lifted a fly ball to shallow right field and Jose Tartabull made the catch. Berry raced home as Tartabull, never known for having a strong arm, made a high throw to the plate. Elston planted his big left foot to block the plate, leaped high to make a one-handed catch and, in the same motion, made a sweeping tag on Berry. When umpire Marty Springstead called Berry out, the game was over. Eddie Stanky, the Chicago manager known as The Brat, argued to no avail. Elston was the hero of Boston, and a picture of the play ran in all the papers.

"When I jumped for the ball, I wasn't thinking of blocking the plate," Elston recalled. "I was just trying to get the ball down quick, but his foot came right into the tip of my shoe, and it kept him from getting into the plate."

Said Dick Williams, "You've got to credit Ellie Howard. The throw was too high and a little off line. Howard grabbed it and leaped down on Berry."

"That play in Chicago, he jumped up and blocked the plate," said Reggie Smith. "That was the turning point for us. We came home that night and Logan Airport was mobbed."

The White Sox won the second game that day, but not before Stanky incited a near-brawl with a few brush-back pitches. According to Smith, Elston always played hard against Chicago because Stanky was the manager. There were only a few people that Elston never liked, but there was some bad blood when it came to Stanky. "I've never hated many people in this game," Elston told the press afterward, "but I don't want anything to do with that runt. And you can quote me on that."

I came up to Boston for the final weekend. The Red Sox, Twins, Tigers, and White Sox all had a chance to win the pennant. The Tigers had four games with the Angels. The White Sox fell out of contention on Friday when they dropped a doubleheader in Kansas City. The two games at Fenway between the Red Sox and Twins were crucial. "We were facing some good pitchers," Reggie Smith recalled. "Elston kept everybody focused on what we needed to do. When he spoke, you listened. He could tell a little joke, smile and tell you one thing. Then he'd give you a look; he had one way of speaking matter of factly and you knew it was time to be serious. That was Elston."

Yastrzemski was unbelievable that weekend. He earned his MVP Award with ten hits in his last thirteen at-bats. The Red Sox rallied to win on Saturday. On Sunday, Yaz went 4-for-4 on the last day of the season as Lonborg won his twenty-second game in a 6–3 victory over Minnesota. After the final out, the fans raced onto the field. Elston calmly trotted out to the mound, shook Lonborg's hand, and calmly walked away from all the craziness.

"I told Elston that day about a dream I had the night before," Reggie Smith said. "I knew we were going to win. In the dream I saw fans pouring over the fences. After we won, I saw Elston leaving the field as soon as possible. . . . No doubt Elston helped us win it. We were a young team. Our average age was about twenty-six. We needed someone like Ellie to show the way. He brought the Yankee aura of winning to the Red Sox. He was like a pitching coach to Lonborg, Gary Bell, Gary Waslewski, Lee Stange, guys like that. He knew how to call a game. He knew things like who the really big hitters were, how to pitch to them, what pitch to call."

Still, the Red Sox had to wait for the outcome of Detroit's last game. If the Tigers won, there would be a playoff in Detroit. If they lost, the opening game of the World Series would be that Wednesday in Boston. The scene in the Boston clubhouse was tense. The champagne was on ice. Players stayed in their uniforms listening to the game from Detroit on the radio. Some played cards. When Dick McAuliffe hit into a game-ending double play and the Tigers lost, the clubhouse went crazy. Tom Yawkey was in tears. Everybody was all excited. Someone asked me why I wasn't, but he didn't realize I had been through this nine times before.

The trade to Boston turned out to be a blessing. Boston was a great city, and the people there appreciated Elston and gave him credit for helping the Red Sox win the pennant. The Impossible Dream had come true, and Elston was going home to St. Louis for his tenth World Series.

CHAPTER SIXTEEN

Retirement

To this date, I have never seen anyone have a season like Yaz had, but we don't win it without Elston.

—REGGIE SMITH

I MET BILL VEECK WHEN I WAS IN HIGH SCHOOL. HE OWNED THE ST. Louis Browns, and he came to Vashon High School to speak to our assembly. I got up and asked him a question about the economics of bringing a black ballplayer to the major leagues. Mr. Veeck was well loved by the black community in St. Louis. He was very active with black people; he brought baseball to the streets. He knew that black athletes were not treated fairly. I always thought if any owner were to hire a black manager, it would be him. That's just the way he was. He was innovative and fair.

Indeed, baseball history would be entirely different had Mr. Veeck named Elston as major-league baseball's first black manager. We were in St. Louis for the 1967 World Series when Elston got a phone call from Veeck, who at the time was trying to buy the Washington Senators. We agreed to have breakfast at the Jefferson Hotel. I came along and heard the whole thing. I asked Veeck if he remembered the question I asked him in high school, and he said, "Oh, yeah, sure," but I know he was just saying that to be nice. As we talked over breakfast, I couldn't believe my ears. Veeck wanted Elston to manage his baseball team. When he asked Elston if he would like to try managing, Elston laughed and said, "Would

I like to finish this breakfast and go on breathing?" Elston was so excited. He and Veeck shook hands and agreed that Elston would be his manager starting in 1968. The only catch was that Elston would have to wait until the deal went down before he could tell anyone.

Of course, Elston never got to manage the Senators, or any other major-league team. James M. Johnston was the chairman of the board in Washington, but he died a few weeks later and his executor decided he could find another buyer who was offering more money than Veeck had in mind. The club was sold to a group headed by Bob Short, who eventually moved the Senators to Texas after the 1971 season.

Actually, I blame it all on the other owners. They are such dogs. They didn't want Veeck back in baseball. When he owned the Cleveland Indians and Chicago White Sox, Veeck came up with some crazy ideas to promote baseball. Other owners never liked the gimmicks he came up with—cap day, exploding scoreboards, a midget pinch-hitter. In 1942, when Veeck tried to buy the Philadelphia Phillies, he was intent on breaking baseball's color barrier. With the help of Abe Saperstein, the man who ran the Harlem Globetrotters, and black sportswriter Wendell Smith, Veeck hired twelve black players to play for the Phillies. Kenesaw Mountain Landis, the racist baseball commissioner, got word that Veeck was intent on integrating the Phillies, and Veeck soon found out that the National League had taken over the team. Later, Landis arranged for the Phillies to be sold to William D. Cox, a man Landis later kicked out of baseball for betting on games. Shortly after he spoke at Vashon High School, Veeck signed Satchel Paige and brought him to St. Louis to pitch for the Browns. I loved Satchel's motto: Mind over Matter. He always used to say, "If you don't mind, it doesn't matter."

Elston would have been the perfect manager for Washington. Of course, Washington's large black population must have been a factor in Veeck's decision to hire Elston, but that's OK. The Senators were always a lousy team. No one could blame Elston if the Senators continued to be losers for a year or two. It would have been a valuable experience and formidable challenge for any manager.

Had the Red Sox defeated the Cardinals in the 1967 World Series, it would have been a perfect ending for Elston's playing career—against his hometown team, no less. It was his tenth World Series in thirteen years, but it was not one of his best. Boston lost Game 1 to Bob Gibson, but the Red Sox, with Elston behind the plate calling a masterful game, won Game 2 as Jim Lonborg pitched a one-hitter. Boston lost Games 3 and 4, but Elston was the hero of Game 5. With the score 1–0 in the ninth inning and right-hander Jack Lamabe pitching for St. Louis, Elston came to the plate with the bases loaded. Instead of sending up a pinch-hitter, Dick Williams surprisingly let Elston hit for himself. Elston delivered a bloop single to right field. Soon after, the Red Sox were on their way back to Boston for Game 6 with a 3–1 victory.

Boston won Game 6, but Gibson beat Lonborg in Game 7. Elston had only two hits in the seven games and had trouble trying to throw out Lou Brock, who stole a World Series–record seven bases. Writers kept bugging Elston about stopping Brock. Elston shook his head and said, "Just keep him off the basepaths. It's the best way I know." The writers also asked him if he was ready to retire. Elston gave them a definite maybe.

After fifteen hundred games, fifty-four World Series games, and nine All-Star Games, Elston, soon to be thirty-nine years old, didn't know if there would be a fourteenth season in the majors. Had the Red Sox won, he probably would have triumphantly announced his retirement and waited for Veeck to name him as player-manager of the Washington Senators.

We headed back home to Teaneck, and Elston spent the next few weeks waiting for the phone to ring. The phone call he wanted never came. The Red Sox called him before we left for Puerto Rico on vacation in early December. They assured him that if he came back to play the '68 season, a coaching job would be waiting for him. The Yankees also were waiting for Elston. If he had retired, I think they were ready to offer him a scouting job or a position coaching in the minor leagues. But Elston didn't want to go there. Yogi Berra never did. Why should he?

That winter, Elston was busy marketing a new invention called the On-Deck batting doughnut. Everybody thought it was Elston's idea, but actually the batting doughnut was the idea of Frank Hamilton, a construction worker from nearby Bergenfield. In the summer of 1967 Frank took his idea to Louisville Slugger. They liked it, but Frank was told to get himself a partner, someone with a name in baseball. At first Hamilton thought about contacting Carl Yastrzemski, but he decided to stay local. So one evening Frank got in his car and showed up, unannounced, at our doorstep with the batting doughnut. Elston answered the door and Frank said something like, "How would you like to make a million dollars?" Elston laughed and invited him in. They went into the basement and talked for about an hour or so.

Elston loved the idea. For years, baseball players would loosen up by swinging two or three bats while they waited for their turn at bat. With the doughnut, now they had a nifty, five-to-ten-pound cast-iron ring, coated with plastic, which easily slipped right over the barrel of the bat. Each doughnut came with a set of directions since it also served as a training device to build up the upper body.

"It helps loosen you up," Elston told the *New York Times* in early 1968. "You slip it on when you're on the on-deck circle. Instead of swinging two or three assorted bats like warclubs, you swing your own bat with the added weight. It slips right off when you go up to the plate and then your own bat feels as light as a toothpick. I gave one to Mickey Mantle and he likes it. I gave one to Willie Mays and he wants twelve more for the other guys on the San Francisco club."

Elston took the doughnut into our basement that winter and used it for hours. He and Hamilton decided to team up with another man named Vince Salvucci, and they went into business together, calling themselves On Deck. When Frank went back to Louisville Slugger, he brought Elston along, and they signed a long-term distribution deal with the world's largest bat manufacturer. As part of the deal, they needed to recruit major-league players to use them. The first team they approached was the Athletics, who had just moved to Oakland. It was Frank's job to sell the doughnut to Joe DiMaggio, who was working for Oakland owner Charley Finley at the time. Elston told Frank that DiMaggio was someone who didn't like to spend money. "Be careful when you talk to him," Elston joked. "He's one cheap son of a gun." DiMaggio at first wasn't interested, but that was before Frank told him the A's would be supplied for free.

Soon after, the A's were using them. Elston lined up player reps from each major-league club. Roger Maris, about to play his final season for the Cardinals, signed on to help promote it nationally. The batting doughnut sold by the thousands, retailing at three to five dollars. Little League, high school, and college teams were buying them up. By the end of the 1968 season, every major-league club was using the weighted batting doughnut. Well, almost every club. White Sox manager Eddie Stanky, Elston's old-time enemy, threw them out in Chicago when the White Sox weren't winning. But Stanky was fired in midseason and Al Lopez, his replacement, immediately ordered a new supply.

Elston and his partners should have made a fortune, but they didn't. In 1972 On Deck was sued by a softball-league umpire in Minnesota. The doughnut was not designed for softball bats, but some softball player put it on his bat and it went flying off and struck the umpire. On Deck lost the lawsuit, but insurance covered that. It took them more than two years before they got a patent, one that was good until 1987. In the meantime, other companies, namely AMF and Adirondack, began making them, too. When AMF started making them, Frank called them on the phone and threatened to sue. They laughed him off. But then Frank put Elston on the phone; that got them to stop. Soon after, a Japanese company came over and expressed interest. Elston and Frank gave them the red-carpet treatment, took them to dinner and a few ball games. Elston and Frank gave them some of the batting dough-nuts to take back to Japan. A short time later Dick Stuart, the former major-league first baseman known as "Dr. Strangeglove," called Elston from Japan and told him that someone over there was mass-producing doughnuts by the thousands. Soon after the Japanese version began flooding the American market.

Elston and Frank hired a patent lawyer named Joe Gasz, but by then it was too late. The market was saturated, and all they could do was make a cheesy settlement that cheated them out of millions.

Thanks in part to the success of the batting doughnut, Elston was determined to play one more season. "I'm not washed up," Elston told the press in early January. "If I thought I were, I would have quit after the World Series." The Red Sox offered him a sixty-five-thousand-dollar contract, a thousand dollars more than he had received the year before. Dick O'Connell said Elston would be worth it if they got a hundred games out of him behind the plate. The way Elston felt that spring, he figured he was good for 125. His bad elbow was never 100 percent, but it didn't seem to be a problem.

Most of Elston's teammates were elated that he was returning. Well, almost all of them. A young catcher named Mike Ryan popped off before spring training. He came right out and said he didn't want to play second fiddle to Elston Howard, or any other catcher for that matter. It didn't take long before the Red Sox traded him off. It made Elston think of the days when he had to play behind Yogi. Imagine if Elston had said that about Yogi? Not once did Elston ever demand to be traded, though believe me, there were times I told him he would be better off with another team.

I think the reason Elston came back in 1968 was that his .178 batting average for 1967 had hurt his pride. He knew he was capable of producing better statistics. And let's face it, the Red Sox were favored to repeat as American League champions.

True, the Red Sox had a good chance, but there was concern about the pitching staff. Jim Lonborg, the team's young ace, had broken his leg in a skiing accident. There was also concern that Tony Conigliaro might not be able to recover from his awful eye injury.

Elston looked around the American League that spring and saw lots of talent. "Chicago is stronger. They have got a good power hitter in Tommy Davis and a fine shortstop in Luis Aparicio," he said. "Minnesota gave up Zoilo Versalles but picked up pitching and catching. Detroit's got a good pitcher in Dennis Ribant. And Baltimore is no sixth-place team."

Then he looked at the Yankees, who had finished in ninth place in 1967. "You know what kills the Yankees?" he said. "It's the infield. Imagine what a pitcher Mel Stottlemyre would be if he got some decent support."

Elston loved and respected his teammates in Boston; that was another reason he came back. On the road he roomed with Reggie Smith, and I adored him. Elston told me Smith was going to be the American League's best center fielder. Lonborg, Elston said, was the best pitcher in baseball. Elston also got along well with George Scott, a big guy from Mississippi who always made him laugh. But Elston never got used to all of his swearing. Every other word out of Scott's mouth was mother this and mother that. Elston told me about the time they were on a bus in Chicago and he and his teammates decided to count how many times Scott would use that word on the ride to the hotel. When they got there, someone told George that he had used that word fifty-five times. George looked around at everybody and said, "You're a mother-bleeping liar."

Elston worked hard and enjoyed a good spring training, but I personally had no fun in Winter Haven. After being in Fort Lauderdale all those years, it was quite a comedown. The hotel was not on a beach, but in the middle of an orange grove. There was nothing there. There was Cypress Gardens, the local tourist trap, but once you saw the water skiers, that was it.

When the season started we rented an apartment in a Boston hotel and I would take the kids up there for homestands when they were not in school. It was a nice place, not far from Fenway Park. Benjamin Spock, the baby doctor, lived there, too, and that was about the time he was getting arrested constantly for protesting against the Vietnam War.

Yes, 1968 was an awful year, full of tragedy. I remember the Red Sox opened the season in Detroit shortly after Martin Luther King was assassinated. It was a sad day for us because I remembered the time we were supposed to spend the night at his house back in the late 1950s. In Detroit, there was all sorts of rioting. On TV, you could see the place was being burned down. Elston called me and said he could see the flames from the ballpark. He got out of there just in time.

It soon was apparent the Red Sox were not going to repeat as American League champions. Lonborg never made it back completely from his leg injury, and Conigliaro did not regain full sight in his eye. Scott, who hit .303 in 1967, was benched routinely because he was overweight, and hit just .176. Joe Foy also found his way into Dick Williams's doghouse and was traded away. Rico Petrocelli was unhappy. Elston got off to a decent start, and Williams offered to name him to the American League All-Star team. But Elston turned down the chance because our daughter Karen needed an operation.

Karen was about eight years old at the time, and the cerebral palsy was causing her to become spastic. She wore braces on her legs to help her walk, but her leg muscles would tighten up. She was seeing a specialist at New York University Hospital who recommended surgery to ease the pressure on her leg muscles. In retrospect, I wish she had never had that operation. For what the results were, it wasn't worth the time. Karen stayed in the hospital for a week. When she came home we had a physical therapist come in three times a week to help her with stretching and walking exercises. She was good about doing that most of the time. She had such a beautiful spirit. She was handicapped, mentally and physically. But we loved her very much and took her everywhere. One year we drove cross-country to Los Angeles. We put the wheelchair in the back and just went. We loved making that trip. She was so energetic and socially very bright. There was no way of knowing how much pain she had to endure. So many times we would take her to hospitals for checkups. Just the sight of a hospital would cause her to cry.

After the surgery, Tom Yawkey and his wife were very kind to send Karen all sorts of games and toys. But from that point on I know Elston was somewhat distracted, and his game suffered. His bad elbow flared up again and he began having trouble throwing runners out. One day he stood in front of his locker and held his arm out, clenching it as if he were unable to straighten it out. "I heard something clank in my arm on a pickoff throw a few weeks ago," he told Dave Anderson of the *New York Times*. "The next day it was like this. I had bone-chip surgery a few years ago when I was with the Yankees and the doc's not going in there again. If he has to go [in and operate], that's it, I'll retire."

Elston played in only seventy-eight games in 1968 and rarely got into the lineup after August 1, when it was obvious that Boston was going nowhere. Looking back on the season, there were many reasons why the Red Sox didn't win again, and certainly one of them had to be a lack of communication between Dick Williams and his players. Williams would talk at or talk about his players, but he would never talk to them. He was nothing like Ralph Houk, who had no problems communicating with his players. Watching Williams up close that year was a valuable lesson for someone, like Elston, with managerial ambitions.

Elston's career ended on a Friday night in Boston, in the same ballpark where his Yankee career had begun in 1955. He never forgot the standing ovation he received that night. Elston finished the season with a .241 batting average, five homers, and 18 RBIs. Baseball expansion was about to bring to life two new American League teams, the Seattle Pilots and Kansas City Royals, but Elston knew he would not be protected by the Red Sox in the expansion draft. No way would he go that route. Who knows, if they had the designated hitter back then, maybe he could have stayed on.

Of course, I began to have my own thoughts about Elston's future. A few clubs called and asked if he would be interested in coaching or scouting, but Elston told them no. Someone from the Cardinals called and asked if he was interested in becoming a broadcaster. But baseball desperately needed a black manager. About 50 percent of the players were black, so wasn't it about time?

On October 21, 1968, it became official. Elston went back to Boston and announced his retirement. Two days later, there was a big press conference at Yankee Stadium. Frank Crosetti, the long-time third base coach, had announced he was leaving the Yankees. All of Elston's old friends were on hand. Houk was there. So was Whitey Ford. Elston was making history again, this time as the first black coach in the American League.

CHAPTER SEVENTEEN

Good-bye, Jackie

Elston Howard always brought a sense of dignity wherever he went. Never needed to brag, always cool. The first time I met him, I was awestruck by his presence.

—REV. JESSE JACKSON

ELSTON'S PLAYING DAYS WERE OVER, BUT RETIRED HE WAS NOT. IN THE spring of 1969, he was happy to be back in Yankee pinstripes, this time as the first black coach for an American League team. In 1967, when Elston was traded to Boston, Ralph Houk and Lee McPhail had indicated there would be a job waiting when his playing days were over. When Frank Crosetti left the team, Dick Howser, a journeyman infielder who had played the '68 season with the Yankees, was given the coaching job at third base. Elston, who took over at first base, told the Yankees that he was still in playing shape. If an emergency came up, he would be able to catch.

Elston had an ulterior motive in taking the coaching job. Suppose Ralph Houk stepped down? Elston was ready to be Yankee manager, if so needed. It had happened for Yogi after the 1963 season; why couldn't it happen to Elston? Make no mistake, Elston's heart was set on being a big-league manager. The Yankees did ask him to take the managing job at Binghamton, a Class AA team in the Eastern League. Elston was not interested. Why go to Binghamton, 150 miles north of Teaneck, when he could live at home with his family, ten minutes from Yankee

Stadium? The sportswriters said he needed to manage in the minors. Elston disagreed. "This is the big ball club," he said, "and the majors are the only place to be."

Immediately after the 1968 season, one of the owners of a team in the Dominican Republic called and asked if Elston would help put a team together for the winter league down there. The team played its games in San Pedro de Macorís, a town now famous for having produced a number of major-league players, including Chicago Cubs slugger Sammy Sosa. Elston agreed to go, but we thought of it as a vacation. They flew us down to Santo Domingo, and it took Elston about a week to get the team together. Jesse Gonder, the former Yankee backup catcher, was one of the star players. While we were there we were aware of the political climate. One night we went to a party at the house of a general with the odd name of Pettis Pettis. It was one of strangest parties we'd ever attended. All the soldiers outside were carrying rifles, and all the generals inside were wearing sidearms as they were eating and drinking. Guns were everywhere. It was like eating at a munitions factory.

That winter we also saw Haiti, the only black-run country in the Western Hemisphere. There was poverty and begging everywhere we went in Haiti, but the marketplaces were full of color and the artwork was absolutely wonderful. I had never seen so much art featuring black figures. At home, most of the artwork depicted white characters. We loved Haiti. The food was a mixture of Creole and French, two of our favorites. We stayed at a big hotel in Port au Prince with lots of rooms named after celebrities. It was there we met Geoffrey Holder, the actor who laughs as well as he talks. He, too, was quite interested in Haitian art. We went out to dinner one night and he asked me to dance. Can you imagine dancing with Geoffrey Holder? It was fabulous. Hah-ha-ha!

We were so impressed by Haitian art that Elston and I brought a lot of it home. Many of our friends were awestruck and expressed great interest in our sculptures and paintings. That's when we decided to open up an art gallery. About a week later we went back to Haiti, spoke to some art dealers, and figured out a way to bring more Haitian art back to New Jersey. That spring we opened a gallery on Palisade Avenue in Englewood, the next town over from Teaneck. Daisy Batson, one of our old neighbors from our days living on Howland Avenue, knew some things about framing and art history and she agreed to help us run it. Haitian art became big. It was featured in the *New York Times*. Some critics didn't care for it; it featured lots of animals and market scenes, but many of our friends and customers loved it, particularly the sculptures, which were marvelous and sold well. In addition to Haitian art, we sold works by other painters, notably Leroy Nieman and Pablo Carreno. Pablo was one of our favorites. Elston saw a portrait Pablo did of Roberto Clemente and called him up one day. We commissioned Pablo to do one of Elston, and to this day it still hangs on our living-room wall. Pablo did other ballplayers—Roy White, Sparky Lyle—and even did one of George Steinbrenner. For three years, our gallery did quite well, until the recession hit. Our accountant called one day and said we'd better close. People don't buy art when times are tough.

The rest of Elston Howard Enterprises was doing quite well, thank you. In addition to the On Deck batting doughnuts, we had several other business interests. Frank Orechio, a friend of Gil McDougald's, invited Elston to head a division of his travel agency, Group Travel, which catered to corporate travel. During the off-season, Elston would sign off on letters to different organizations, hoping to get big companies to sponsor trips to Europe or Caribbean cruises. Often Elston was the leader, or star attraction, of these groups, and I was more than happy to go along. In 1969 we went to Europe for the first time.

Elston also became partners in a printing business. Big Julie Isaacson, who organized tour groups to the casinos in Las Vegas, would invite Elston and other sports celebrities out to Las Vegas, all expenses paid. It was there, on a junket in which people would pay to play golf and attend dinners and parties with sports stars such as Elston, that we met Lionel Reison, quite a gambler, who had lost practically everything he owned. Reison talked to Elston about joining him in the printing business. Elston was still very popular in New York. It was Lionel's idea that Elston would go around to the Fortune 500 companies and hit them up for business. We opened up a shop in midtown Manhattan and called it Elston Howard Printing, a subsidiary of Sandy Alexander. It did quite well. Elston also became actively involved in starting an interracially owned bank based in Teaneck. Known as the Home State Bank, it was incorporated in 1973 to provide progressive financial services, particularly to the black community. Elston was proud of his role in its development, serving as vice chairman of the board.

A few years later, in 1976, Elston became a partner in the Elston Howard Sausage Company. They had a concession stand at Yankee Stadium, and our daughter Cheryl got her first part-time job working there. She hated it. We had a lot of sausage in our refrigerator, but the company never caught on, and it lasted only a few years.

Elston was very big on the banquet circuit. I don't think he ever turned down a chance to speak to kids. He attended Little League dinners and clinics, and he was a national board member of the Babe Ruth League. He also found time to serve as a volunteer school board member in Hackensack, and one year he helped settle contract talks with the teachers.

In the meantime, because of our daughter Karen, I was heavily involved with the Bergen County Cerebral Palsy Foundation in Ridgewood. There always seemed to be a charity benefit somewhere, and I did as much as I could. I did several fashion shows with Yankee wives to raise money for various charities, and I served as the advertising manager. We would put out a program at each show, and my job was to line up the sponsors.

Even though Elston was now a coach, I still considered myself to be a Yankee wife. I would sit in the stands with the players' wives, but attitudes and fashion were changing. In the '60s, we would come to the ballpark all dressed up in our best clothes. In the '70s, ballpark apparel became less formal, more laid-back. Men hardly ever came to the ballpark dressed in jackets and ties. More of the wives were wearing blue jeans and dressing down, so I had to cool it.

Over the years, I got along well with several of the Yankee wives. Joan Ford and Lucille McDougald were always very nice. Carmen Berra was the greatest dresser. She was the chic-est; her outfits were always so fabulous. There was Bill Skowron's wife, Virginia. We never saw much of her after Bill found out she was cheating on him, and that turned into a messy divorce case just as the Yankees were about to trade him to the Dodgers after the 1962 season. Bobby Richardson's wife was something else. She and Bobby were always very nice and extremely religious. You would sit next to her at a game, somebody would hit a home run, and everyone would cheer. She would turn toward me and ask, "Have you been saved?" I would nod my head, say "yes," and she would go on with her sermon.

Socially, we were out there. There were lots of dinner parties and all sorts of events. I was involved with the Doll League, a group of prominent black women who did charity work but were better known for their parties. They would honor celebrities such as Dick Gregory, Nancy Wilson, and Clyde Otis, the songwriter. One year they gave Diana Ross the Living Doll Award, and Cheryl made the presentation. There always seemed to be a party at one place or another. The place to be was a big restaurant owned by our friend, Sid Allen, over in Englewood Cliffs. When Neil Armstrong walked on the moon, there was a big party that day, and we were there.

At the ballpark, the Yankees continued to struggle. Mickey Mantle had retired, and the team finished the 1969 season with an 80–82 record. On September 23, the Yankees were in Boston when Dick Williams was fired. Immediately, the press began to speculate that Elston would be the next manager of the Red Sox. At the time, Elston was doing a nightly radio show for WLIB, a black-owned AM station in Harlem; he always took a tape recorder on the road to do interviews and then he would send the tapes back to the station. That particular night he interviewed Tom Yawkey and let him know he was interested in managing. A few stories appeared in the papers that Elston was interested in the job. A few weeks later, the Red Sox promoted Eddie Kasko, their third-base coach, to manager.

As coach, Elston got along well with all the young players, some of whom had once been his teammates. Bobby Murcer was back from the army and often consulted him about hitting. Jerry Kenney did, too, and he would tease Elston about the way he dressed, saying that he led the league in blue shirts. "Ellie loved his ties," said Bill Robinson, a young outfielder. "He was a very meticulous dresser. Very clean."

Elston made quite an impression on young Bill, who was traded to the Yankees in 1967 and immediately billed by the press as "the black

Mickey Mantle." He had grown up in Elizabeth, Pennsylvania, and went to Pittsburgh in 1960 to see Game 6 of the World Series, the same game in which Elston broke his hand.

"I never saw him angry. Elston was the consummate professional," said Bill, who now runs a baseball academy just outside Philadelphia. "When I was struggling my rookie year and had millions of reporters around, he and Mickey Mantle would always say 'you gotta be yourself.' That helped a lot though I was only twenty-three and it was obvious I was too raw to play in the majors.

"He was a very classy, classy man. That first year with the Yankees, me and my wife were invited over to the Howards for a dinner party, and there were all these beautiful people there, wearing shark skin suits, minks, furs, there was caviar, everything. I was wearing my first hundred-dollar suit and my wife was wearing a fifty-dollar dress. We just sat there and took it all in."

Unfortunately, Bill Robinson never made it with the Yankees. He was no black Mickey Mantle. He batted only .206 in New York, though later he matured into a productive outfielder who played for many years in the National League. In the spring of 1970, Bill was called into Ralph Houk's office. "We were in Fort Lauderdale," he recalls. "I knew something was wrong because Howser and Ellie were in Ralph's office. When they told me they were sending me down to the minors, I started crying and Ellie was crying, too. He told me to be myself and everything would work out. I thanked him for everything he did for me." Years later, when Bill Robinson won a World Series ring playing for the Pittsburgh Pirates in 1979, he began wearing his World Series ring on the same finger as his wedding ring—just like Elston.

Surprisingly, the Yankees suddenly got a lot better in 1970 and won ninety games, finishing in second place behind the Baltimore Orioles. Under the direction of Mike Burke, the Yankee president, there was new optimism. I liked Burke a lot; he was an interesting person. I know he was Irish and his family had money, but he always had that old WASP look about him; you know, frayed around the collar. One year Elston was being honored by friends back in St. Louis. Mike Burke was asked to send a Yankee representative to be there. Mike not only went himself but also chose to stay in a local motel instead of one of the big hotels downtown. Burke had some promising players on the Yankees, Bobby Murcer, Roy White, Mel Stottlemyre, Jerry Kenney, but he never had the resources to put the team over the top. Back then there was no free agency, no great prospects in the farm system, no George Steinbrenner. The Yankees were still owned by CBS, and for years they played with the same hand they were dealt back in 1964 when they purchased the club from Dan Topping and Del Webb. Maybe things would have changed for the better had Curt Flood won his case against baseball's reserve clause. We were pulling for him. Flood was really the unsung hero of the century. Funny, but no one seems to remember what it was like before the days of free agency. He was right; you were really like a slave when you played major-league baseball. You had no control over your own life. We would see Curt every so often when we went back to St. Louis. He, too, was a fabulous artist, and I loved discussing art with him. I admired him as an excellent ballplayer, a sensitive human being, and a brilliant artist. He died in January 1997. For what he did, every ballplayer should get down on his knees and thank Curt Flood. Like Elston, he never got his due. He is responsible for what baseball is today.

In 1970 came *Ball Four*, in which Jim Bouton took baseball publishing to a new low, writing a book that often depicted his former Yankee teammates as a bunch of jerks. Today, I will have nothing to do with the man. For whatever reason, he took a number of cheap shots at Elston, the man who was his catcher when he was a twenty-one-game winner in 1963. Like most of the Yankees, Elston was really ticked off when he heard about Bouton's book. When Elston was traded to Boston in 1967, he got a number of calls from several magazines and publishers, asking him to rip the Yankees. Elston turned them all down. We didn't need that kind of money. Later, Bob Gibson called him up and said Bouton was "knifing you for blood money." Elston became so angry at Bouton that one day he called Bernie Miller of *Gentleman's Quarterly*. Elston asked him to help write a rebuttal. It was going to be a book called "Foul Ball."

"Jim Bouton is a very self-centered and selfish man," Elston told Joe Durso in the *New York Times* in July 1970. "During the two years he was a winning pitcher with the Yankees, he was one of the cheerleaders.

Then he stopped winning and he stopped cheering. He got angry at the Yankees because they traded him even though they carried him for three years after he'd stopped winning. And believe me, he couldn't pitch then, he was hopeless. He didn't miss any bats at all. No matter what he says, he wrote in anger. You can picture him all you want as a daring guy who told all. But he's just frustrated."

At no point in *Ball Four* did Bouton mention the fight he had with Elston. "He's been angry at me ever since I decked him in the West Point gym one day," Elston recalled. "We played exhibition games against the Cadets, the Yankees and Mets rotate each year. We always go early for a little basketball in the gym. This day, I guess it was 1963, Marshall Bridges . . . put on the gloves with me, then hopped out of the ring and gave everybody a big laugh.

"Then Bouton challenged me. I weighed 220 and he was only 180. But he insisted on fighting. I hit him twice and he went down. He used to challenge guys on everything. Even Bobby Richardson, who was a very religious man. Now, you just don't go around arguing with a man's beliefs. A couple of times on the team bus, I had to keep Joe Pepitone from hitting him."

In his book, Bouton said Elston hit him with a body block when Bouton had an argument with Frank Crosetti. Elston disagreed. "He got KO'd in the second inning in the first game of a doubleheader, then sat in the stands. He was called into the locker room and Frank Crosetti balled him out. He wrote about that in the book. But he wrote that I threw a body block on him when he and Cro started shoving. Believe me, if I had thrown a body block on Jim Bouton, he would have hit the wall. It just didn't happen."

Another thing Bouton said was that Elston would rub mud on the ball for Whitey Ford. Even Whitey will admit to some degree that was true. "But he forgot to write how I used to rub the ball for Jim Bouton, too," Elston said. "He just has this inferiority complex where guys like Whitey Ford and Mickey Mantle are concerned."

Bouton accused Elston of anonymously backstabbing manager Johnny Keane in the press and then making a big scene of sticking together during a team meeting. "Clete Boyer called me up long distance the other day and said in all the time he was assistant player rep, he never remembered a meeting like the one Bouton described in the book, where I was supposed to have jumped up waving my arms because some player had criticized Johnny Keane. Nobody remembered that."

On the heels of Bouton's book came a tribute from Richard Nixon. President Nixon, whom I met once in 1978 at a Yankee game, was a big baseball fan, and somebody thought it would be a good idea to have him pick his all-time baseball team. With the help of his son-in-law, David Eisenhower, he selected all-star teams for the American and National Leagues for both the pre– and post–World War II eras.

"As any baseball fan will understand," said Nixon, "I found it impossible to limit the team to nine men. Consequently, on each team I have selected two catchers, five starting pitchers, one relief pitcher, and five additional infielders and outfielders who are listed as reserves." Elston and Yogi Berra were named as catchers on the postwar American League team.

The funny thing is that Nixon may have voted for Elston, but Elston never voted for him. In 1968, Larry McPhail, the father of the former Yankee general manager, called the house, looking to enlist Elston among a group of black athletes, namely Jackie Robinson and Wilt Chamberlain, who would publicly endorse Nixon for president. He didn't know Elston and I were Democrats, so I told McPhail there was no way he would do that. He got very upset and hung up the phone on me, saying something to the effect, "for all the things I did for Elston."

Hah!

In May 1970, one night after a game against the Tigers, there was a car crash in the Bronx. Elston was hospitalized with severe head and face cuts. Three people in the other car also were slightly injured. It was amazing it wasn't worse. Elston's car was struck on the passenger side, spun around, and struck a light pole on the driver's side. It was demolished. Dazed by the crash, Elston climbed out from the wreckage, the police report said, and walked two blocks to Morrisania Hospital. X-rays showed no fractures, but he was treated for shock and kept overnight. Police said Elston's two-door red Mach 1 was turning west onto 167th Street from the Grand Concourse's northbound center traffic lane. He was trying to avoid the traffic home by taking a shortcut. He stayed in the hospital for two days.

In 1971, the Yankees hired Bill White, making him baseball's first black broadcaster. Everyone was so proud of him. Over the years we had seen Bill quite a bit starting from the days when he played with the Cardinals, then in spring training at St. Petersburg, and later whenever we went home to St. Louis. When Bill came to the Yankees, he knew little about the American League players. So Elston naturally was the first person he went to that spring training. Elston had some broadcasting experience himself, having worked as a color analyst on local high school football games in 1969 for Channel 11. In fact, he turned down an offer to work with Jack Buck doing St. Louis Cardinals games. "Elston made my job much easier because he had great knowledge of the players," says Bill, looking back. "He knew what they were doing that year, what positions they would be playing, things like if they were coming back from injuries. Elston knew all that. I had to depend on him. He was my eyes and ears on the field."

It wasn't long before Elston and Bill became good friends. He and his wife, Mildred, had five kids of their own; they owned a farm out in Pennsylvania, and we would bring our kids down there. Bill and Mildred were very active; they liked to play tennis and do some skiing, and the kids could swim and play together for hours. Everybody would always have a good time. Elston and Bill sat together on plane trips and dined out often. Elston loved to order steak. He always ordered it "Pittsburgh"—charred on the outside, red inside. Bill was quite a joker, always teasing Elston about something or another. Frank Messer, Bill's broadcast partner, tells a story of how the two would carry on while playing cards: "Bill said to Elston, 'You've been with the Yankees so long, you're beginning to think you're white.'" Retorted Elston, "You can kiss my butt at noon in front of Macy's store window." Elston and Bill spent years talking baseball, where it was at in terms of race, why there were no black managers, no blacks in the front office. It didn't take Bill long to realize Elston's dream. Being the first black manager was secondary. Elston just wanted to manage.

In 1972, Jackie Robinson became particularly vocal in his criticism of baseball owners and their tendency to hire the same white managers over and over again. That fall, before he threw out the first pitch of the World Series, Jackie let it be known that Elston, Junior Gilliam, and Frank Robinson were willing and able. Elston had always admired Jackie, and he appreciated his support.

In the late '60s, everyone knew Jackie was having personal problems at home. His son, Jack Jr., had come back from Vietnam with psychological problems, and when his son died in 1971 in a car accident, Jackie became another person. Jackie was always a very proud man. You never saw him with his head down. But when his son died he was a different man. He was losing his eyesight. More important, he was losing his interest in life.

Looking back, I consider myself lucky that I had a special relationship with Jackie, with both of us being diabetic and sharing the same doctor. Whenever I would see him at dinners or parties, I would try to talk to him as much as I could. In 1968, when his son was arrested for buying drugs, I wrote him a letter to tell him how much we thought of him, how much we appreciated everything he had done for civil rights. He wrote back, and I still have the letter:

Dear Arlene and Elston:

I am sorry to have taken so long to answer your nice letter. As you must know we have been very busy trying to help Jackie get straightened away. We feel real good at this stage. While his problem is serious, he is in great shape with a good attitude. He must overcome some anger, but that will come. The past few weeks have been somewhat of a nightmare but we believe our family is strong enough to overcome. It was tough at first but we forgot about what people would think and made up our mind we can't help what goes on in the minds of other people when Jackie is our main concern. We have given of ourselves and we believe we are gaining a son. Sometimes a problem can be an asset. We feel strongly this is happening to us.

I guess the training and coming season will be tough but Elston's drive will make him a great asset to the younger fellows. I wish you the best as well I can only hope things continue to go well.

Please be assured we appreciate your taking the time to write. It's a good feeling knowing people care and your letter has helped us during a difficult period. Thanks so much for doing so.
Sincerely, Jackie and Rae

In 1972, shortly after he threw out the first pitch at the World Series in Cincinnati, Jackie died. Elston and I were saddened by the news, and we received a special invitation to attend the funeral, at Riverside Presbyterian Church in New York, which we did. The next day there were newspaper photos of Elston standing solemnly as Jackie's casket was carried out of the church.

Jackie's death hit Elston hard. Elston had idolized him since the day in 1947 when he decided that like Jackie, he, too, would play professional baseball for the Kansas City Monarchs. In spirit, Jackie Robinson was the big brother Elston never had. He was a big brother for all of us.

CHAPTER EIGHTEEN

Ready to Manage

*If humility is a trademark of many great men, with that as a measure,
Ellie Howard was one of the truly great Yankees.*
—GEORGE STEINBRENNER

I FIRST MET GEORGE STEINBRENNER AT SPRING TRAINING IN 1973,
just a few weeks after he had purchased the New York Yankees from CBS
for something like ten million dollars. My first impression was that he
was rather young to be a baseball owner. Elston was forty-four years old,
and we thought it was odd that he was a year older than the new owner
of the team. I had read all the newspaper stories that called Steinbrenner
an "Ohio hayseed" coming to New York. The New York press was really
against him. They hated the idea that someone from Cleveland, of all
places, was coming to New York to own the Yankees. But the Yankees
needed some new blood and new direction, and I could see right away
that George was committed to making the Yankees winners again.

One of Steinbrenner's first moves as Yankee owner was to hire Gabe
Paul to run the team. Back then, no one had any idea that George would
break the record for firing managers. Ralph Houk was still managing the
Yankees in 1973, and Elston was in his fifth season as his first-base coach,
with Dick Howser coaching third. Houk always admired Elston's character and spoke often of his great baseball sense. "He was smart," Houk
said. "Just because a batter couldn't hit a curveball, say, Ellie wouldn't sit
back there and call for a curveball all the time. He knew how to mix up

the pitches. He was well liked by players on the other clubs. So that once in a while he'd get pretty good information that way. You know, maybe this guy's got a bad leg, or something like that. He's always looking for that type of info."

Tony Kubek, then an analyst for NBC's "Game of the Week," also thought Elston had great baseball savvy. "Elston would have been a great manager," he said. "He knew baseball inside and out. He knew how to think. He was a student of hitting. He knew which stadiums were the worst to hit in. He knew the players on the other teams. He knew how to handle pitchers. It's a crime he didn't get to manage."

Other teams also appreciated Elston's skills as a communicator and role model. During the 1973 season, the Cleveland Indians, actually it was Rocky Colavito, telephoned Elston and asked him to have a motivational talk with George Hendrick, a young outfielder with a reputation as a slackard. Elston turned down the offer. "I am a Yankee," Elston said. "I don't want to get mixed up in another club's problems." When Hendrick was fined for not hustling, Elston said he thought the fine was too small. "He's a real dog," Elston told a reporter. "You could see the way he played against us. Half trying. What a shame. All that talent going to waste." Elston said that about a lot of players.

In 1973, the American League introduced the designated-hitter rule. Elston said that for him, the DH rule had arrived five years too late. The Yankees got off to a good start that season but fizzled after the All-Star break, finishing with an 80–82 record. The last game of the 1973 season, October 1, was a crazy night. Everyone knew that it would be the last game in the old Yankee Stadium, which would be closed and torn up for two years of renovation. Before the game was over, fans were ripping up the seats and taking them home. In fact, Elston himself later brought home a couple of box seats from the old stadium; we still have them in our backyard. Before that last game, Houk called Elston and the other coaches into his office for a pregame meeting. Houk shocked everybody when he said he was resigning after the game.

"I couldn't believe it," Elston said later. "I said, 'You've got to be kidding.' But he said, 'No, it's a fact.' I told Lanier about it when Hal got a hit late in the game and he was on first base. Believe me, he was stunned.

It was the same in the clubhouse after the game when Ralph told the team, and he broke up a bit while doing it. The players felt the same way, too. As they went into his office for their last good-byes, I felt the same way. After all, I've been with Ralph a long time, both as player and coach."

Immediately after the game, word got out that Houk had quit, and there were people who were saying that Elston was going to get Houk's job that very night. As I was waiting with our friend Bernie Miller for Elston outside the locker room after the game, people would walk past and ask me what it was like to be the wife of the new Yankee manager. I was delighted. Maybe it was true. Maybe the time had come. Maybe Ralph Houk had put in a good word for Elston and something big, something historical, was about to happen. But it didn't happen that night; it didn't happen at all. When Elston emerged from the locker room, I expected to see his big old smile, but he was expressionless. When we got out to the car, we thought maybe he was going to tell us the big news, but he said very little. We told him about the rumors and learned that they were false.

Nevertheless, it didn't take long for Elston to begin campaigning for the Yankee job he wanted so badly. Now he thought he finally might get his chance. For the first time, Elston threatened to leave the Yankees. There was an opening in Detroit, where Billy Martin had been fired. "I'd be a pioneer for my race, being the first black manager," Elston told the *New York Post.* "I don't know anything about the situation in Detroit, but if I received an offer, I would go." Uncharacteristically, he called Detroit to talk with Jim Campbell, the Tigers' general manager. Elston went to see Yankee team president Lee McPhail and Gabe Paul and actually dared them to name him Yankee manager. Elston was told that he was "on the list."

"I told Mr. Paul that I would like the job. I said to him, 'If you're ready, I'm ready.' He told me he would mention it to Mr. Steinbrenner that I was interested.

"Ralph Houk and Jim Turner, the pitching coach, helped me an awful lot. Turner particularly taught me so much about handling pitchers, which is the most important thing in managing. I think baseball should be ready for a black manager now. There won't be any problems with the ballplayers. There are so many blacks in the game now. Not the way it was when I came up, just a couple on every team."

Lee McPhail promised the Yankees would have a new manager in place by early December. "During the World Series we will find out who's available. We want a winner. The new manager could come from within or outside the organization. Everybody will be considered. Yes, everybody."

Baseball still had no black managers in 1973. Frank Robinson was thirty-eight years old and still making $160,000 playing for the California Angels. Frank said for the "right offer" he could be talked into retirement. When he heard that the Yankee job was open, he jumped into the race. Someone asked him if he would take the job. "New York would be a great place to start," he said. "I'd like it."

Besides Frank Robinson, there were other capable black candidates, including Junior Gilliam, Maury Wills, Tony Taylor, and Bill White. Although Bill liked being a broadcaster, I think it's a shame no one ever asked him to manage. He would have been a great manager. Bill thinks Elston would have been a good manager, too. He believes, and I agree, that had CBS not sold the Yankees and had Mike Burke remained Yankee president, Elston surely would have been hired to succeed Ralph Houk. When Burke ran the Yankees, it always seemed that they were acting like great white liberals. It would have been the thing to do. "When Mike Burke hired me as a broadcaster, he made a social statement," Bill said. "Gabe Paul would have hired a baseball manager simply for baseball reasons, not to make a social statement. Mike Burke would have hired a manager and also made a social statement.

"I knew Ellie wanted to manage. He should have. He had as much experience as anybody out there. . . . There is no reason he couldn't have been a manager. He was quiet, not an extremist in any way. He did his job, didn't rattle cages. His private life was exemplary. Lots of times when they talked about blacks as managers, they'd find something off the field to rip apart. Elston had the perfect marriage and the perfect family. No reason he couldn't have been chosen as a manager."

Red Smith in the *New York Times* said Elston was the obvious choice to become the next Yankee manager. "The devout hope here is that Elston Howard succeeds Houk," he wrote. "Authority sometimes changes a man unpredictably, but it says here that Howard has the temperament, experience, judgment and personality to fit the job. He was an outstanding player with the disposition and intelligence to realize his full potential. He has always enjoyed great personal popularity without sacrifice of dignity or privacy. He was the first black player on the Yankees and the first black coach in the American League, but the Yankees shouldn't give him Houk's job just so they'll be the first team in the majors to have a black manager. Neither should they deny him the job for fear they might someday have to be the first to fire a black manager. Sooner or later all managers get fired. Until that time came for Elston Howard, soon or late, he would bring the Yankees something no team can ever have too much of, nor any individual. That's class."

But Dick Young in the *Daily News* saw things differently. "I can't tell you who's going to manage the Yankees, but I can tell you who isn't. Elston Howard isn't and it's not because he is black. Mickey Mantle isn't black, and he won't get the job either. The common denominator between Ellie and Mickey is experience. The Yankees want a man who has been there."

By December, it was apparent that the new Yankee brain trust was interested in someone else: Dick Williams. After his firing by the Red Sox in 1969, Williams became the manager in Oakland in 1971 and led the A's to three straight division titles and two World Series championships. But right after the 1973 World Series, Williams abruptly resigned. It was said he could no longer take the day-to-day meddling of Oakland's controversial owner, Charlie Finley. Now he was ready to work for George Steinbrenner? But Finley wouldn't have it. When the Yankees announced just after the World Series that Williams would be their next manager, Finley set up a legal roadblock. Williams was under contract for two more years in Oakland. To release Williams from his contract, Finley said the Yankees would have to give up Fritz Peterson, one of their best pitchers.

Meanwhile, Elston spent weeks waiting for a phone call that never came. He announced to a reporter, "The phone number in New Jersey is Teaneck . . . heck, they know it." The reporter asked him if there might be some reservations about major-league players playing for a black manager. "There might be some awareness, but not on my part. I don't care what a player's color is, black, white or purple. It's a player's job to produce and hustle. I like winning."

Shortly after 1973 turned into 1974, Elston got a call from the Yankee front office. He was told the next manager would be Bill Virdon, Elston's teammate back in 1953 with the Kansas City Blues. Virdon, who beat out Elston for the International League batting title by two percentage points in 1954, and who played center field for the Pittsburgh team that had somehow upset the Yankees in the 1960 World Series. Now it was Virdon who was taking Elston's dream job away.

Looking back on those days, Bobby Murcer said he was pulling for Elston. "I wish Ellie had been named the manager," he said. "He would have been excellent. The knowledge that he had, the way he treated people, he would have been absolutely perfect. You know what they say about catchers: that they make the best managers. I wish it had been Ellie."

On January 3, Elston and Whitey Ford were asked to attend a big press conference at Shea Stadium, where Virdon was introduced as the new Yankee manager. It hurt Elston to go, but he did. In the papers the next day, Virdon was photographed wearing a Yankee uniform and flanked by the smiling faces of Elston and Whitey, who was named pitching coach. Virdon had been fired as manager of the Pirates during their September stretch drive. It was said he had been dismissed because he had lost control of the team, particularly after he had a fistfight with his third baseman, Richie Hebner. Now, here he was to manage the Yankees.

As it turned out, Bill Virdon was a very nice man, and Elston enjoyed coaching for him. Some of the New York media just laughed when he got hired, seeing him as an "interim" manager. George Steinbrenner seemed intent on hiring Dick Williams, who had filed a suit to get out of his contract with Finley. "No, I can't say we've abandoned the idea of signing Dick Williams," Steinbrenner was quoted as saying. "If he gets free, we'd have to cross that bridge if we come to it." Virdon said he did not see himself as an interim manager. "I'm not concerned about Dick Williams," he said the day after he got the job. "I realize I am on the spot in accepting the Yankee managership."

Elston didn't get the Detroit job either. Surprisingly, Ralph Houk got it. The decision to pass Elston over was just another tired excuse. "What do I have to do to manage?" he said to me. "Why do I have to be better than everyone else?" It was just another slap in the face.

CHAPTER NINETEEN

Elston Jr.

The expectations were too high for my brother. He became a walking time bomb.

—CHERYL HOWARD

THE HARDEST THING ABOUT BEING THE SON OF ELSTON HOWARD WAS the name itself. Even when Elston Jr. was a baby, there were expectations. As his mother, I had my own expectations of what he should be, what he could achieve, but the world assumed he would follow in his father's footsteps and be a baseball player. He tried his best, but often it just didn't work out.

Being Elston Howard Jr. had its advantages and disadvantages. On the one hand, he loved being the son of a famous Yankee ballplayer and often got special attention. Some kids wanted to be his friends just because of that. On the other hand, he sometimes had to deal with envy and jealousy, and he was teased unjustly because of who he was.

In Little League, everyone expected him to play baseball for no other reason than that he was the son of Elston Howard. He was just a little kid, and so much was expected from him. He was supposed to be a super kid even though he was only six or seven years old. Everyone would ask him, "You gonna be a catcher like your dad?" "No," he would say almost defiantly, "I don't want to be a catcher. I want to be a pitcher." It was his first declaration of independence.

Elston went to his son's games whenever he could. Sometimes he would sneak into the ballpark and watch from the outfield so that he would not draw attention to himself or make Elston Jr. nervous. Whenever Elston Jr. would pitch and see his dad in the stands, he would get nervous, try too hard, and sometimes lose control. It was like that for years. I always thought he was terrific as a baseball player, but he was never a natural like his dad. Elston Jr. was a good-natured kid growing up, but he was never inclined to work very hard at developing his baseball skills. As a Little Leaguer I thought he was as good as any of the other kids. He was a very good pitcher; he seemed to enjoy it. "I won't forget the first day out for the Little League team," he told a newspaper writer in 1968. "Everybody was saying, 'Wow, he must be great because of his father.' They made me captain right off."

Elston Jr. loved to spend as much time as he could with his famous dad. What time they did spend together never seemed to be enough. Elston tried to teach his son the same lesson he had learned growing up in St. Louis: To succeed, you must be better than anyone else. I don't think Elston Jr. ever could grasp the reality of that, or of what his father had gone through. Early on, the two of them got along well. They would talk about all sorts of things, but schoolwork was the thing Elston liked to talk about the most. He always wanted to make sure his children were doing their best in school.

Elston Jr. tried to keep up with his dad's career, and he was proud of Elston's accomplishments. He was eight years old when Elston won the MVP award in 1963, and I had to explain to him why all the kids in the neighborhood were making such a big fuss about it. Still, Elston Jr. had other interests. Once when we were at home and the Yankees were on TV, Elston hit a grand slam, and I ran into the other room to see if Elston Jr. had seen it. He was watching *Hogan's Heroes* on the other station. "I felt so dumb," Elston Jr. would say later about that night.

There were times when Elston Jr. seemed more interested in things other than baseball, notably electronics and airplanes. When we made him take piano lessons, Elston would say, "Look at Denny McLain. He's a pitcher who flies his own plane, plays the organ, and makes lots of money." He and his father built some model airplanes and would take them over to a place in Teaneck on Degraw Avenue, near Hackensack, where they could fly them. Elston Jr. also had a set of trains he was very fond of. He had fish tanks. He loved to fish; he and his father would go to a nearby reservoir. Cheryl would go, too. Cheryl, two and a half years younger than Elston Jr., had other interests. She took to the arts. Right away we saw she had the talent to be a performer, so we encouraged her. She took ballet lessons and later modern dance. She and I frequently went to the theater together, even the opera.

One of Elston Jr.'s best friends growing up was David Gordon. They became buddies at the nursery school I took Elston Jr. to in Englewood. The owners of the school were Jewish, so he met several Jewish children such as David and became very friendly with them. He didn't have any problems being the only black in his class, except that the color of his skin made him somewhat different. One of the cute things was the time he went to David's house for dinner. One of his parents told me they were having a conversation about school when David said, "You know, Elston is different. His hair is curly." Everybody dropped their spoons.

When he went to school, all the kids knew who his father was. He never had trouble until 1963, when we moved into our new house. Some of the kids began picking on him. Neighbors from across the street came to me and said, "Your son started a fight with my child, what are you gonna do about it?" Elston Jr. would never admit that it was the other kids who started it, but we knew who was calling him names and who was doing the pushing and shoving. And then these people would have the nerve to blame me for it!

Growing up in our household was difficult for him. With his father spending so much time on the road with the Yankees, he learned to accept his role as the only man in the house. Attention was hard to get, especially with his baby sister Karen being handicapped. She got all the attention, and although Elston Jr. loved her dearly, I think there were times when he felt ignored or forgotten. Sometimes he and Cheryl would fight over the most insignificant things. He always complained that I took Cheryl's side, but I was not going to let him beat up on his little sister.

Aside from his bouts with Cheryl, he was never one to fight and seldom made trouble for his teachers at school. He had some really good friends in high school, some really nice boys. There was one incident when he was fifteen or sixteen. I went to Florida; his father was away, and I had a housekeeper stay at our home for a couple of weeks. Elston Jr. had a few of his friends at the house, and they went downstairs to the bar we have in the basement and had a few drinks. When we got home, we found several empty bottles at the bar. They didn't have the sense to throw them out. Maybe a bottle or two of champagne, some hard liquor. We had to find out who the boys were and tell their parents. We were horrified that Elston Jr. would do something like that and had a big discussion with him. He and his friends were barely old enough to drive.

Elston Jr. loved going to Yankee Stadium, where he was treated royally, and he got along well with other Yankee kids, notably Bobby Richardson's son, Robby. For years, there were no other black players on the Yankees who had children. Whenever they would have family days at the ballpark, he was the only one. Some of the other kids had never seen a black kid before. I think it was one of Yogi's kids who once asked me, "Is he black?"

Elston Jr. liked it when the Yankees would let him go on the field and practice. When his dad got traded to Boston in 1967, Elston Jr. was eleven years old. He loved going up to Boston on weekends. Sometimes I would send him up there on the train by himself so he could be with his dad. He knew all the players; Carl Yastrzemski was one of his favorites. So was Reggie Smith. They became pen pals. Reggie was like the big brother he never had. "He was just a good kid," Reggie Smith recalls. "We weren't that far apart in age. Elston was always so proud of him; that he was going to school. He was always encouraging him."

When Elston came back with the Yankees, Elston Jr. took a liking to Thurman Munson, who had a similar interest in becoming an airplane pilot. Elston promised to get Elston Jr. lessons at Teterboro Airport for his fifteenth birthday, and he later became a licensed pilot. At Teaneck High School, Elston Jr. lettered in football and basketball as well as base-ball. In football, he played split end. I'm not sure how much he enjoyed it or if he thought it was expected of him. His grades were just so-so. He was lazy, and we had to stay on him to do his schoolwork.

The hardest part had to be the heckling. If he dropped a fly ball, someone would yell out, "Your dad wouldn't miss that," or "Stick to catching." "Once I lost two games in a row in high school and I cried and cried and told Dad I wanted to quit baseball and do something else, cake-making, anything," he told a newspaper reporter in 1978. "He always said it would be tougher for me. He didn't push me, but I always knew it meant so much to him for me to play."

At 6–3 and 185 pounds, he resembled his father. But Elston Jr. never wanted to wear number 32 like his dad. Instead, he chose 25. He was a good outfielder and pitcher (he was 8–0 in his senior year), but when it came time for college, the scholarship offers didn't come rolling in. He wanted to go to Arizona State, but his grades were not good enough. Elston absolutely wanted his son to go to college, and he offered to help in any way he could. So he called a friend of his, Ron Frasier, who was baseball coach at the University of Miami, and they got him into school down there without a scholarship.

In 1973 the Vietnam War was winding down, and we didn't have to worry about him getting drafted. I used to say the Vietnam War was such a horrible, unfair war. Too many young black men were going over there and losing their lives. The whole war was such a disgrace. If my son had been drafted, I would have insisted that he go to the draft board and sign up as a conscientious objector. I saw what happened to Jackie Robinson's son; I didn't want the same to happen to our family.

In the fall of 1973, Elston Jr. left home for the University of Miami. When he tried out for the team, the local TV stations came out to see him play. He hurt his arm, was red-shirted, and eventually he flunked out. He came home and got a part-time job. While he was in Miami he befriended a pitcher on the team named Steve Lerner, an outspoken young man who had grown up in Miami Beach. "Ellie learned to play baseball as a New York Yankee," Lerner said in a *Miami Herald* article in 1976. "He comes on lazily, like he's a non-competitor. He learned from guys who can slip on a banana peel and look graceful. But he never was quite good enough to learn how to dive and get dirty and make the great catch, and he suffered greatly for it."

Elston Jr. stayed home in 1974 and enrolled at Bergen Community College. Lerner called him up in August of 1975 and told him that he was transferring to Dade Community College's downtown Miami campus in an attempt to find more playing time and perhaps get drafted by a major-league team. He invited Elston Jr. to join him. So our son again packed his bags and headed back to Miami, where he was housed by the Lerner family.

Charles Seager, the baseball coach at Dade-Downtown, told Elston Jr. that he needed to hit .300 in fall practice or he wouldn't make the team. He didn't hit .300, but none of the coaches had the nerve to cut him. "He didn't seem to have a good attitude and seemed to be having a hard time adjusting," Seager said. "Still, I liked the way he swung the bat." Elston Jr. batted .307 with five home runs that season. He played right field on a team that won the Southeastern District title with a 48–8 record and advanced to the junior college national championships in Grand Junction, Colorado. Whenever he struck out, there were people in the crowd who would yell out at him, "What's your name?" At season's end, he was hoping to get drafted by a major-league team, but the call never came. His father could have helped him get a minor-league contract, but Elston Jr. wanted to do it on his own.

About this time, the father-son relationship became strained. Elston became distressed that Elston Jr. was getting bad grades and apparently was doing a lot of partying. Whenever they talked, they began to argue.

Elston became quite critical, and told his son he had to do better. Elston Jr. became defiant. The expectations were becoming too much, and he became rebellious.

By now, Elston was curious to see if his son had major-league potential. So he phoned Mike Ferraro, the manager of the Yankees' Class A farm team in Fort Lauderdale, and arranged for a scout to take a look. A few weeks later, Elston got the following report from Steve Souchock of the major-league scouting service, dated May 5, 1976:

This boy has some raw talent, has great power to right center. As good as you or the Moose. He can hit it long way out there. He hits about 85 percent of his balls to right center. Talked to him and suggested that he try pulling everything in batting practice and even if the ball is inside, out of the strike zone, just try and throw the bat at the ball and hit it foul to left. Game time do what comes naturally. Bat at this time is on the slow side and can't handle balls in on him. Bat will have to generate more bat speed. If he works on it I believe he will have a chance, as the saying goes, if you can hit, they will find spot for you.

His actions are little slow and stands flat footed in outfield that is correctable with some work and think he can speed up his actions some if he really wants to pay the price and go to work on these things. If he will work on these things this summer and has another year at school down here, then I would say he has a chance to be drafted next January.

In the summer of 1976, Elston Jr. stayed in Miami and got a job working for the city parks department. He came back for another year at Dade and hit .375 with seven home runs. Again, he was not drafted. Eventually, he came home, and we had a family talk about what he should do next. It was decided he had to try college again. We got him into the University of Alabama. Mel Allen, who knew some people down there, called and recommended him. Alabama was looking for black athletes, and Elston Jr. knew Coach Seager, who had gone there to get his doctorate.

In the fall of 1977, Elston Jr. went to Tuscaloosa and majored in marketing. When he tried out for the baseball team, he was the only black player on the squad. "Being the only black on the team, there were no problems," he said in 1978. "I had never been to Mississippi before last year, so I told all the guys to call me 'Carlos' when we went there to play."

George Steinbrenner knew that Elston Jr. was at Alabama, so he kindly arranged an exhibition between the Yankees and the Crimson Tide at the conclusion of spring training 1978. On April 6, 1978, Elston saw his son play right field for the Crimson Tide. Elston was so proud. He told Elston Jr. that Catfish Hunter was gonna "lay one in there" for him. But Elston Jr. went hitless that day. He was too nervous. Playing in front of his father always made him that way.

Alabama had a 23–20 record that season. Elston Jr. hit only .230 and had just 18 RBIs. It was very disappointing. Opponents began wondering if he really was Elston Howard's son. He came home unhappy and played that summer in the Cape Cod League. Occasionally he would hang out at Yankee Stadium and get a first-hand look at the Bronx Zoo Yankees.

"They didn't think anything about me being there," he told a reporter in 1978. "They knew I wouldn't blab. And if I did, it would be only to Dad. They know my father is cool. He's the only one they go to with a lot of their problems. He's a go-between for Billy [Martin]. Last year he was the link between Billy and Reggie [Jackson]. He could communicate both directions."

Elston could have pulled the strings to get his son a tryout, maybe even a minor-league contract with the Yankees. Elston Jr. was always adamant. He said no. Elston wanted his son to play baseball. Elston Jr. felt he had to make it on his own or not at all. There was no other way, he felt. If he couldn't do it without his father's help, he wouldn't do it at all. "That wouldn't be right," he insisted. "No matter what happens, I'll always feel that way."

In the fall, he decided not to return to Alabama. Now twenty-four years old, he stayed home, got a day job, and enrolled at Bergen Community College to take a few night courses with the intention of getting a degree. He did that for a few months, but he was arguing with everyone in the house. He was very unhappy. He felt like a failure, that he had let everyone down. And so one morning, without telling anyone, he got up, packed his car, and was gone. All he left was a note.

Elston was deeply hurt. He knew Elston Jr. was a good ballplayer, a good son. He could see his son working harder, earning his degree, and becoming a major-leaguer. Elston Jr. playing major-league baseball in a Yankee uniform would have been his dream come true. Instead, his son's abrupt departure left him with a broken heart.

CHAPTER TWENTY

Yankee Class

*I will never forget that laugh. It was contagious. He was a fun-loving
guy with a serious side.*

—GOOSE GOSSAGE

ON A GLORIOUS, SUNNY DAY ON APRIL 8, 1975, ELSTON LOOKED ACROSS
the field at Cleveland's Municipal Stadium and saw baseball's first black
manager. The Cleveland Indians, the first American League team to sign
a black ballplayer in 1947, were breaking ground again. For Elston, there
were mixed emotions. In some ways it was like a race to see who would be
the first, and naturally Elston was disappointed to have lost. Then again,
he was proud of Frank Robinson and secretly cheered for him that day
when the player-manager homered in his first at-bat off Yankee pitcher
Doc Medich. Give Frank Robinson credit; he campaigned hard to be
baseball's first black manager. Elston did not campaign as hard.

After the 1973 season, Elston thought his turn might come. While
the nation was becoming entrenched in the Watergate scandal, the San
Diego Padres appeared to be moving to the nation's capital, and Elston
was approached about being their manager. C. Arnholt Smith, owner
of the Padres, was forced to sell the team. A group headed by Joe Dan-
zansky, the head of a grocery-store chain known as Giant Food Stores
in the D.C. area, made an offer to buy the Padres and move them to
Washington in time to start the 1975 season. Two names surfaced when
it appeared the Padres were going to hire a new manager for their move

to Washington—Elston Howard, and Maury Wills, the former Dodger shortstop who was a Washington native and NBC baseball commentator.

On a plane to Milwaukee late in the 1974 season, Elston took a seat next to a young left-handed pitcher named Mike Wallace. Elston liked him and thought he had pretty good stuff. But Elston knew that Wallace wouldn't be back with the Yankees next season, and he asked him if he would like to pitch in Washington. "He saw the handwriting on the wall," Wallace recalls. "He knew I wouldn't be back. Elston was a very serious baseball guy. He was a winner who didn't accept failure. When he asked me if I wanted to pitch in Washington, he was recruiting me to play for him. He didn't say whether he would be general manager or field manager. He couldn't say anything about it or it could be considered tampering. Why else would he ask me?

"When you think about it, Elston in D.C. would have been a great fit. Very plausible. He didn't just go round flipping his lip. He knew something was gonna happen. But the last minute the hamburger guy pops up."

The hamburger guy was Ray Kroc, the man who made millions from McDonald's fast-food franchises. He came along at the last minute, bought the team from Arnholt Smith, and pledged to keep the Padres in San Diego.

Instead of managing in Washington, Elston returned for another season as the Yankees' first base coach. Bill Virdon was in his second season managing the Yankees. In 1974 the Yankees had played their home games at Shea Stadium while Yankee Stadium was being renovated. They came on strong and finished in second place in the American League East, two games behind the Baltimore Orioles.

In 1975, Elston thought the Yankees would be ready to win their first title since 1964. Gabe Paul, the man Ralph Houk used to call "the Smiling Cobra," was running the Yankees, and he was not shy about making trades. In 1974, Fritz Peterson and three other pitchers were traded to Cleveland for first baseman Chris Chambliss and pitcher Dick Tidrow. Bobby Murcer, one of Elston's favorite players, was traded to the San Francisco Giants for Bobby Bonds. By 1975, Catfish Hunter had left Oakland and joined the Yankees as one of baseball's first high-priced free agents. With Gabe Paul calling the shots, the Yankees, to Elston, looked nothing like the all-white team of the 1950s. For the first time in their history, the Yankees truly had become a team of color. In addition to Chambliss and Bonds, the team roster included the likes of Nate Colbert, Bob Oliver, Sandy Alomar, Roy White, and Elliot Maddox.

Chambliss right away was one of Elston's favorites, and the feeling was mutual. Chambliss had grown up in St. Louis, and his parents had often employed my sister Loyette as a baby-sitter. His father, a navy chaplain, was a contemporary of Rev. Baker, Elston's godfather. Chris always could relate to Elston's story. For years he has been waiting himself for a major-league managerial job. "Elston was my man," said Chambliss. "He was like an older brother to me. He was great to have around. He had a lot of common sense and knew a lot about hitting. He was a good teacher, so positive, always under control. Sometimes when something comes up on the club, I think back and ask myself, 'how would Elston handle this?'"

Chambliss had a good season in 1975, but the Yankees did not. In early August, Bill Virdon was fired and replaced by Billy Martin. Virdon's dismissal left Elston with mixed feelings: He was glad to be reunited with Billy, his old friend and teammate, but once again he was hurt because he had been snubbed for the job he so badly wanted. We loved Billy. At heart, he was a nice person, very generous. Billy's problem was that he was an alcoholic. One time we were in Kansas City for the play-offs; he joined us for breakfast and ordered eggs and scotch. When Billy was drunk he could be a pretty rotten person; he got into fights. But you know what? He never hit a black person. He was a student of Abraham Lincoln and liked to talk about him all the time. He was a rough Italian kid from California, a Frank Sinatra type. There was something charming about him, and I liked him. After Elston died, every Mother's Day he would send me flowers.

In 1975 George Steinbrenner had been banned from baseball by commissioner Bowie Kuhn for making illegal campaign contributions to Richard Nixon's 1972 presidential campaign. About a year later, after he was reinstated, I was flying home from spring training when I ran into George at the Fort Lauderdale airport. When George found out that I was flying coach, he took out his credit card and had me bumped up to first class, in a seat right next to him. We talked about several things that day, our families, the Yankees, but there was one thing I had to ask him: whether he knew how badly Elston wanted to be a manager. "Yes," he said. "But Elston is too good to be a manager. Managers are hired to be fired. He deserves better than that."

Because of the way he hired and fired managers, the way George saw it, if he hired the first black manager, he would be the one to fire the first. That is what he said to me; that he would rather put Elston in the front office. Of course, I told Elston about this, and he wanted to hear nothing more. To him, it was another tired old excuse.

Even after Frank Robinson became the first black manager, Elston thought for sure he would be the second. In 1976, when the expansion Toronto Blue Jays began interviewing for their first manager, Elston campaigned for the job. Elston would have gone back to Toronto. He was still popular up there from his days in the International League with the Maple Leafs in 1954 when he was named the league's Most Valuable Player. Elston interviewed with Peter Bavasi, Buzzie's son, who was the team's general manager, but once again he was left disappointed. The job went to Roy Hartsfield. Another slap in the face.

In 1976, the Yankees returned home to Yankee Stadium and won their first pennant in twelve years. Elston remained a prominent figure in the Yankee clubhouse. As Billy's Bronx Zoo Yankees were taking shape, several of the players took great comfort in Elston's advice. To some, he was the "complaint" coach. Billy's confrontational style didn't sit well with a lot of players, including Thurman Munson. One time Elston reportedly threatened to quit coaching after he broke up a clubhouse argument between Billy and Thurman.

"Elston was a pretty good bouncer," Chambliss recalls. "He could break up fights before they started." "As a coach he was an enforcer, but he had a calming presence," said Ron Guidry, another one of Elston's favorites. "As long as Elston was around, arguments never got out of hand. He was a big man; you didn't cross him. Never."

Then along came Reggie. Elston had always admired his talent, but Reggie Jackson was a showboat in Elston's eyes. Reggie used to kid around with Elston, tease him about the conservative way he dressed, but Elston would always say one word to Reggie: "Class." Thank God Reggie's mellowed, but in those days he was very egotistical, just like Steinbrenner. In 1977, none of the players hung out with Reggie, particularly after he announced to the world that he was the "straw that stirred the drink." The only one who would go out with him was the batboy, and I think Reggie paid him to do that. Elston told me about the time Rev. Jesse Jackson came into the Yankee clubhouse for a prayer meeting and asked Elston if it would be OK to have a talk with Reggie. "He's got problems," he told Elston. "I could help this young man."

Elston's feelings about Reggie came to a head the night the Yankees beat the Kansas City Royals for the 1977 American League pennant. Reggie was going around the locker room, spraying champagne on everybody. Elston was having trouble with his eyes and, according to Guidry, politely asked Reggie to spray someplace else. When he kept on spraying, Elston got off his stool, picked Reggie up, and slammed-dunked him into a garbage can.

"Reggie and Elston never saw things eye to eye," said Guidry. "They were different era ballplayers. Reggie loved the limelight, and that did not appeal to Elston." "Elston was the opposite of Reggie in terms of personality," recalled Goose Gossage, who joined the Yankees in 1978. "Elston wasn't flamboyant in terms of being a professional. He was a true Yankee."

In June of 1977, the Yankees acquired Cliff Johnson in a trade with Houston. On his third day in a Yankee uniform, with the Yankees playing poorly in Boston on national TV, Cliff found out what Elston Howard was all about. "I was in for a rude awakening," Johnson recalled. "The second day in Boston, a Saturday, we were getting massacred again. The Little General [Martin] was about as hot as a steam kettle. I'm sitting on the far end of the dugout when a ball drops into right field and Reggie jogs over, picks it up, and throws it back in.

"Billy blew his lid. He hollered for [Paul] Blair to get that son of a bitch out of there. Obviously he wanted to embarrass Reggie. Reggie came off the field and went right at Billy. Right then I knew I might have to get into the middle of this and break it up. But as Elston and Yogi approached the problem area, I backed off."

As Reggie and Billy began yelling face to face in the Yankee dugout, TV viewers across the country saw Elston step forward between the two men, his face staring solemnly straight ahead. Before any punches could be thrown, Elston grabbed Billy, and Yogi pulled Reggie back.

"I came running and Ellie yelled out, 'Let's cut this out,' " Yogi recalled. "Good thing we broke that up. It was an ugly scene."

Elston was perplexed by the whole situation, Johnson recalls. "He said, 'What's going on here?' He was just as mystified as everyone else."

The whole nation saw the incident, including *Los Angeles Times* columnist Jim Murray, who called for Billy's head on a platter. Furthermore, he urged the Yankees to hire Elston to restore Yankee class. "If Billy Martin is let go and it's hard to believe he won't be I would respectfully suggest to Yankee owner George Steinbrenner that he go down the row of lockers one night until he comes to that of one of his coaches, Marse Elston Howard, a man who, for my money, could run the Yankees the way the Yankees ought to be run—with dignity, a minimum of theatrics or flourish.

"With Elston Howard the pinstripes were already built in. He was an impeccable ballplayer who could play you three positions sometimes in the same game, hit you 28 home runs and bat anywhere from .290 to .348, and never disgrace you in the parking lot. He fit in so well that the militants were beside themselves. They wanted him to break up the furniture once he got in. They accused him of uncle tomming but Elston took his hat off to nobody. Elston was just a born Yankee."

In 1978, a season in which Billy Martin was fired in midseason and replaced by Bob Lemon, Elston was made bullpen coach. Phil Pepe wrote in the *Daily News* that Elston's "demotion" was a shabby way to treat an old hero. Elston went to Billy and asked him why. Billy said it was George's idea. So Elston went to George and George told Elston he was a "god-damn liar." He said it was Billy's decision. At that point, Elston said to just forget it. "I'm not saying it's a racial thing," one unidentified player said in a newspaper, "but a lot of people are going to think it is."

As first base coach, Elston always felt he was a part of the game. In the bullpen, his job was to answer the phone whenever the manager wanted Goose Gossage or the other relievers to warm up. "When he was running the bullpen, he'd go over hitters with you, who's coming up, who might pinch-hit, who's on the bench," said Gossage. "He had knowledge of the game. He was a strategist."

Goose never forgot Elston's reaction when a Boston fan spit in Gossage's face during the 1978 playoff game with the Red Sox. "It didn't bother me; I was so into the game," Goose recalls, "but Elston was about to jump over the fence at the guy. He was standing right next to me when one of the Boston security guys came back to assure him that they had taken care of him."

Elston never backed down from anyone. Frank Messer remembers an evening in Detroit when he and traveling secretary Bill Kane went to dinner with Elston. Messer was on crutches at the time and Kane, who is handicapped, walked with a limp. On the way back to the hotel, they were confronted by a panhandler looking for spare change. Messer gave him a quarter. "But then the man went around the corner and came back at us with two of his friends and threatened us unless we gave them more money. Elston grabbed that one guy by the neck and slammed him into the wall and said, 'You tell your friends to run, or I swear I'm gonna kill you.' Elston was so strong; I never saw a man react so fast. That scared them. Elston let the man go and they all took off running. It was the only time I ever saw Elston mad."

But Elston knew when to have fun. Following one victory celebration, Cliff Johnson had the tables turned on him when he tried to pick Elston up. "I was gonna pick him up, but he got position on me and put me in the tub of ice. He was just goofing around. I didn't think he could do that to me, but he did. Elston was a strong man. Everybody laughed."

One season later, Johnson and Gossage were fooling around in the shower and got into a fight. Gossage's thumb was broken; the Yankees were doomed to a fourth-place finish. Johnson was soon traded away. The fight would never have happened if Elston had not gotten sick. He could have been there to stop it.

CHAPTER TWENTY-ONE

Farewell

I was at his fiftieth birthday party with lots of good friends and teammates. It was a surprise party, but it was obvious that Elston was strained and glum. He told me about the incident at La Guardia.
—BERNIE MILLER, DECEMBER 1980

SOMETHING WAS WRONG, TERRIBLY, TERRIBLY WRONG. THE FIRST SIGN came on February 13, 1979, shortly before Elston's fiftieth birthday. He and several other Yankee team members had gone to Canton, Ohio, to attend a charity dinner in honor of Thurman Munson. Sparky Lyle flew home with Elston, and when they arrived at La Guardia Airport, Sparky went to get the car while Elston stayed back to get the luggage. When Elston bent over to pick up one of the bags, he started to puff. He was out of breath; he felt tired and weak. He couldn't pick up a suitcase.

Elston spotted Sparky's car outside in a no-parking zone. Elston left the bags behind and walked out to the car. "Something's wrong with me," he told Sparky. Sparky drove Elston home to Teaneck. The next day Elston was on his way to see Dr. John Gluck, the Yankee team doctor. He had Elston taken to Lenox Hill Hospital in New York for tests. When the test results came back, the diagnosis wasn't good. The muscles around his heart had become inflamed by a rare virus known as coxsackie. The doctor said it was myocarditis. There was no instant cure. The only medicine, he said, was rest.

Elston spent much of the next twenty months in and out of the hospital. Instead of going to Fort Lauderdale for spring training, he was in the hospital, and there were serious doubts he could make it back for opening day.

Elston came home in time for his fiftieth birthday on February 23. Pablo Carreno, the Cuban-born artist whom we had befriended when we owned the art gallery, invited us to a dinner party at his apartment. Pablo lived in Manhattan in the Chelsea section in a walk-up apartment. When Elston and I got to the top of the stairs, he was clearly out of breath. It was supposed to be a surprise birthday party, but when we entered the apartment, nobody yelled "surprise"; they kept on partying. That was the only surprise. It was still a memorable evening. Pablo served a roast pig, and many of our friends were there with lots of gifts. Sparky Lyle, who had been traded to Texas, bought Elston a big oversized cowboy hat.

Back home and out of baseball for the first time in his life, Elston became edgy. He hated being sick. "I wish I was down there," he told *Daily News* writer Phil Pepe that spring. "I'm going crazy up here with nothing to do. I read every newspaper, including the Wall Street Journal, and any book I can get my hands on. I've done enough reading to last me the rest of my life."

Dr. Gluck said there was little hope Elston would make it back by opening day. "Right now it's indefinite," he said. "I know Ellie's restless and I can understand that. He's been such an active person all his life. But the first thing we must be concerned with is Ellie's health. This kind of thing takes a long time to turn around. There is no magic medicine to cure it. The only thing is complete rest. It might take months; we just don't know. What we're looking for is a general sign of improvement. Even after he leaves the hospital, he will have to continue to rest at home."

Dr. Gluck didn't really know just how serious Elston's condition was. Sometime that summer, he prescribed the wrong medicine for Elston. One weekend, Elston got a funny reaction and became quite dizzy. Dr. Gluck didn't know what he was doing. I had to write a letter to take him off the case. I almost filed a malpractice suit against him.

At the time, even I wasn't sure how serious Elston's condition was, that it would be fatal. Most doctors back then didn't know much about coxsackie. Dr. Nicholas DePasquale did, and that's why he became Elston's number-one doctor. He was the chief cardiovascular surgeon at Lenox Hill and locally at Holy Name Hospital in Teaneck, and he had done some research on it. He said athletes generally have enlarged hearts and are more prone to that type of virus. He knew how sick Elston was. "I'll never forget what Dr. DePasquale told me," Elston said. "He told me, 'You're lucky to be alive.'"

George Steinbrenner called and assured Elston that his coaching job would be waiting. Thanks to George's kindness, Elston never missed a paycheck. "Don't worry," Steinbrenner told the *Daily News*. "Ellie will be taken care of. We all want him back as soon as possible. But we also want to be absolutely sure he's completely recovered before he comes back. The main thing is his health."

At home, Elston was under house arrest. He could not go outside; no swimming, no exercise. A few friends and ballplayers came to visit. A neighbor, Hazel Shorter, brought in board games, puzzles. Occasionally he played Chinese checkers or tended to his gun collection. He would sit all day and play his jazz records. He had a great collection: Miles Davis, Quincy Jones, Frank Sinatra. And he watched television. "I watched all the Yankee games," he told the *Daily News*. "And if they weren't on, I watched the Phillies and the Red Sox on cable." As for me, I didn't mind Elston watching the baseball games on TV, but after a while, all the football and basketball got to me.

Without Elston in the clubhouse, the Yankees struggled for much of the 1979 season. They did not repeat as champions of the American League East, finishing in fourth place behind Baltimore. In May the clubhouse fight between Goose Gossage and Cliff Johnson upset him. "I'm always one of the first guys in the shower," Elston told the *New York Times* shortly after it happened. "And when I was in there, Goose and Cliff were usually in there, too. All they would have needed was for someone to yell "hold it" and they would have realized what they were doing." Elston, being Elston, made a keen observation about the Gossage-Johnson incident: "When two guys can fight and nobody thinks about their color, that's something."

At one point, Elston attributed his illness to overworking himself in the weight room. "I was overextending myself on the Nautilus exercise machine," he told the *New York Times* at Thanksgiving of 1979. "I used to go to the stadium last winter and work out with Chris Chambliss, Bucky Dent, Willie Randolph, and Yogi Berra's son, Dale, and I remember one day I had a blowout. I couldn't do ten arm pumps. I had to stop at six." Elston said his illness was worse than a heart attack. "After a heart attack," he said, "a doctor wants you to exercise. I couldn't exercise."

Fans sent get-well cards, flowers, and fruit. Thurman Munson and even Reggie Jackson called every once in a while, but no one called more than Yogi Berra. "Yogi called about twice every week," Elston told the *New York Times*. "Many people don't realize how close Yogi and I are. Yogi is one of the nicest guys in the world."

In August came news that Thurman Munson had died in a plane crash. It was so very shocking and sad. The Yankees chartered a plane to take everybody to Ohio for the funeral. I went, but Elston could not go. Diane Munson said she knew Elston was too weak to attend. Elston and Thurman always got along well. The week before Thurman died, they took a nice photo together that I still have upstairs in Elston's trophy room.

For years, Steinbrenner had tried to coax Elston into accepting a front-office job. On February 14, 1980, shortly before his fifty-first birthday, Elston was appointed assistant to Steinbrenner, making him the highest-ranking black man in the American League. "I'll be an assistant to the Boss," Elston told the *New York Post*, downplaying his illness. "I don't have a title yet, but George convinced me to give up coaching to take this job because he said anybody could be a coach but not anybody could get to be an assistant to the owner of the most important team in baseball.

"I guess this move makes me the Jackie Robinson of the Yankee front office," he joked. "When the season starts, I will be with George and I will work with our scouts and I'll visit our minor-league clubs. I'll be learning all aspects of the baseball business."

As another spring training rolled around in 1980, Elston was to become more involved in Yankee affairs; he even took a short trip to Florida. The Yankees had traded Chris Chambliss, but signed Bob Watson to take his place at first base. Bob and Elston became good friends, and Elston helped him find a new house here in New Jersey.

Elston was able to make a few appearances for the Yankees as Steinbrenner's right-hand man. Steinbrenner would ask him to speak at dinners or visit minor-league ballparks in the Yankee system and judge the talent. Steinbrenner had become famous for trading away young Yankee talent. That spring Elston was sent to Greensboro, North Carolina, to evaluate a prospect from Indiana named Don Mattingly. Elston was very impressed. According to the *Daily News*, Elston reported to Steinbrenner that Mattingly was "a major-league prospect and it would be a mistake to trade him." Years later Mattingly told me himself how impressed he was when Elston met his family and took them out to dinner.

Elston was quite happy that Dick Howser had been named manager for the 1980 season after George had fired Billy for the second time. He and Dick had become good friends since beginning their coaching careers together back in 1969. Under Howser, the Yankees began winning again, and Elston credited Steinbrenner for building a strong organization.

"George Steinbrenner spends the money, you see," he told a newspaper writer that summer on a scouting trip to Norfolk, Virginia. "Just a few years ago the Mets were the dominant team in New York. They were not only piling up money, we were playing at Shea Stadium while Yankee Stadium was being renovated, and they were getting all the concession money. It looked like they would be the number-one team in New York for years to come.

"But they wouldn't spend. George did. He built a winner with free agents, and he stocked the farm system. A lot of people knock him, but here's a guy who wants to win desperately. He hires people and he asks them, 'What do we need to do to win?' And when those people tell him, he goes and does it. You should see the pitchers we have coming along, big guys 6–6 or so, who throw hard. I don't have anything but good things to say about him."

Elston, however, never felt like his old self. Cheryl was singing in a show on Long Island and he really wanted to go see her perform, but he was too weak. No matter how hard he tried to hide it, he was a sick man. His face became puffy from the cortisone pills he was taking. Often his forehead would suddenly become damp with cold sweat. He had no energy, no will to do anything stressful.

At Thanksgiving dinner, he couldn't eat his turkey. He said it was too dry, so I made him some soup. Then he went to lie down and began to complain that he could not breathe. That night I took him back to the hospital. He came home soon after, but his condition only got worse. On December 4, I took him to Lenox Hill for more tests. I didn't know he would never come home again.

Dr. DePasquale knew the end was near. He came to the house one day to say that we might want to consider applying for a heart transplant. He wanted me to think about it. He said it might not be worth it, though. He explained how hard it was to get a new heart and the risk that a transplant would not be successful. For more tests, we took Elston by ambulance from Lenox Hill to Columbia Presbyterian Hospital, where Elston's room was down the hall from the wife of Claus Von Bulow.

Everyone knew Elston's condition was terminal, but no one would say so. We got a call from Dr. Bobby Brown, a cardiologist and Yogi's old roommate who was the American League president. George Steinbrenner called. His father had just passed away. George called me up and I distinctly remember him asking me, "Can't we do something?" Those words were so haunting, but there was nothing we could do.

I went to the hospital every day, sometimes once in the morning and early in the evening. Elston told me about his delirious dreams. There was one in which he was shoveling some snow or coal, and Steinbrenner was saying, "faster, faster." I spoke to the hospital psychiatrist, and he said that such dreams were normal for some people who are close to death.

Elston was pretty miserable. Every day I would bring him the *Daily News*, his favorite sports section, but he had no interest in it. Because he was connected to a catheter, he was very uncomfortable. One of the last things he said to me was, "I don't want to die like this."

On Saturday afternoon, December 13, Elston was taken into the cardiac intensive care unit. The doctor told me Elston's heart was very, very weak. Of all the things that could take his life, how strange that it would be his heart, which was so full of life, so full of love. I called our children and told them to come home right away, that their father was in Columbia Presbyterian Hospital and that his condition was very serious. Cheryl was in Detroit with the road company of the show "They're Playing Our Song." Elston Jr. was in Miami. Our good friends, Fran and Bernie Miller, came to the hospital that evening and sat with me, waiting for the kids to arrive. "Elston was hooked up to a network of life-sustaining equipment," Bernie Miller wrote in his memoirs. "It was an ominous thing to see, an exercise in futility."

Elston Jr. arrived, and he and I went into the room to see Elston one more time. When Cheryl arrived, Elston Jr. told her not to go in. He didn't want Cheryl to see how bad their father looked. Around eight o'clock, we were sitting in the waiting room when a doctor came in and said, "I'm sorry, he's in cardiac arrest." He said there was nothing we could do. It was just a matter of time. We waited around until about 10:30 before we decided to leave the hospital and go home. Once we got home, Elston Jr. decided to go back to the hospital. Then came the phone call shortly after midnight. Elston's heart had stopped. He was gone.

I was so numbed by Elston's death that there was no real way at the time to express my anger. For years, I suppressed it, but not the way that Elston always suppressed his. All the good and bad times that we had been through, twenty-six years of marriage, the endless baseball games, the social problems, raising our kids, it all seems too much. It was hard just thinking about the years he sacrificed for the New York Yankees; he could have played for another team and been a star. Maybe if he had not put up with the racism, maybe if they had made him a manager, he would still be alive today. Don't get me wrong. I consider myself blessed; we had great times together. Still, one thought has become increasingly clear to me: Baseball killed my husband.

Epilogue

On July 21, 1984, the New York Yankees officially retired Elston Howard's number 32 in a ceremony in which they also retired Roger Maris's number 9. In his memory, a plaque was dedicated in center field of Yankee Stadium.

Dr. Nicholas DePasquale helped establish the Elston Howard Cardiovascular Research Fund. Thousands of dollars in donations have helped aid in the research of myocarditis caused by the Coxsackie virus.

Shortly after Elston's death, I assumed day-to-day control of the Elston Howard Printing Company, making it one of the most successful black-owned businesses in the country. I sold the ownership in 1991. Today, I remain actively involved at the Galilee United Methodist Church in Englewood, New Jersey, and am a board member of the Fresh Air Fund in New York City and the Hackensack YMCA. I also remain active in the Yankee organization, making an appearance at Yankee Stadium every year on Old-Timers' Day.

Travis Howard died of complications from prostate cancer in Memphis on October 8, 1988. His funeral was attended by Elston Jr. Our son returned to the family printing business in the mid-'80s before taking a job with Honeywell. He died in 1994.

Cheryl Howard continues to perform professionally. She has appeared in several movies, Broadway and off-Broadway shows, and occasionally sings the national anthem at Yankee games. She sang the national anthem on July 18, 1999, the day David Cone pitched a perfect game against the Montreal Expos.

Karen Howard died from complications of cerebral palsy in 1991. Teannie Edwards continued to coach sandlot baseball. He died in St. Louis in 1985.

Dr. Ralph Wimbish died in 1967. His son is the co-author of this book.

Afterword

by Mike Vaccaro

My father was a Yankees fan, reared on the remarkable teams of the late '30s and early '40s, nourished by the teams that won five champions in a row in the early '50s, emboldened by the teams that won five straight American League pennants to begin the '60s. It's funny: he was a Queens kid growing up, and while the Mets weren't even a twinkle in the borough's eye in those years, most of his friends were Dodgers fans. A few were Giants fans. There weren't many Yankees fans growing up in the Corona section of Queens, which may have only been 10 miles from Yankee Stadium as the crow flies but felt so much further away.

"For me, it was easy," my dad told me near the end of his life. "The Yankees were the ones with all the vowels."

He meant Italians, which to a second-generation Italian-American was a very big deal: Lazzeri. Crosetti. Russo. Rizzuto. Berra. DiMaggio, of course. And Billy Martin, whose name may not have sounded like his family came from the Old Country but whose pride in his heritage was obvious even from the bleacher seats at Yankee Stadium.

Funny thing, though. Whenever someone asked my father who his favorite Yankee was, he never said DiMaggio or Rizzuto. He never said Mickey Mantle or Whitey Ford or Tommy Heinrich, so many of the usual suspects you would expect from a kid who'd grown up in an Italian-Irish enclave. And to him it was never even close.

"When I think of the Yankees," my dad said, "I think of Elston Howard. I think of him being a great player, sure, but I think of the dignity he had his entire career. You could see even from the television that this was a man who loved being a Yankee. He was the one."

Years later, I was spending some time with Yogi Berra at his museum in Montclair, N.J., and we were talking about many things. One subject I'd always wondered: when Elston became a Yankee in 1955, and as he became an All-Star for the first of nine consecutive seasons beginning in 1957, and as he slowly (and then permanently) began to nudge Yogi to the outfield as he caught more and more games (capped by the hard-to-fathom total of 141 games he started at catcher in 1964, when Yogi was his manager), did Yogi ever find himself harboring any resentment toward the younger man? They were both nice men, but even nice guys can have their egos bruised from time to time.

Yogi shook his head.

"Never," he said. "Ellie was the best of us. Your dad had it right."

By now, you no doubt know this as well, thanks to this elegant and eloquent book by my friend, Ralph Wimbish, and Elston's widow, Arlene. You know all about Elston's struggles and his triumphs as a ballplayer, about the wonderful love story that was Elston and Arlene's marriage. And you probably leave these pages equal parts glad for having taken the journey with Elston through his wife's eyes, and somewhat melancholy that we were deprived a fitting closing chapter to his story.

For Elston was only 51 when he died on Dec. 14, 1980. It is only right to wonder what the '80s—and what his 50s—might have held in store for him. It was in the '80s when baseball's own trailblazing history forced the game to re-evaluate where it had evolved in terms of race; in 1987, commemorating the 40th anniversary of Jackie Robinson's break-ing of the color line, Al Campanis made his ill-fated remarks on ABC's "Nightline" that forced a national conversation about the way baseball had been slow to seek qualified African-Americans for management positions. The Yankees, too, were about to enter a turbulent time as an organization. It stands to reason that at some point, had Elston lived, George Steinbrenner would have understood the value in offering Elston a chance to manage his beloved Yankees rather than recycling Martin for a fourth or a fifth time.

Alas, that's one of the great What-Ifs in sports history. We know how revered Elston was among his teammates in New York—and how immediate his impact was in 1967 when the Yankees dealt him to Boston and he became an integral part of the stretch drive toward an Impossible Dream. We know how deeply he affected young players who sought his counsel. Willie Randolph—who would become the first African-American manager in New York City in 2005, a slot that by rights should have been Elston's—once told me, "I don't know that I would have lasted two weeks in New York if I didn't have Ellie to turn to when I was a rookie [in 1976]. Whatever hard times I thought I was going through, he'd been through worse—so much worse—and even if he never told me all his stories he offered me all his strength. I'll never forget that."

And we know that it was Elston, and Elston alone, who stood between an embarrassing moment at Fenway Park in the summer of 1977 escalating into something far worse. When Martin removed Reggie Jackson from a June game against the Red Sox and then promptly got in his slugger's face for a perceived lack of hustle, it was Elston who reminded that even at age 48, he was still a strong bear of a man, pulling Martin away from the fray before the argument could morph into an assault.

"We've all seen that video a thousand times," said ex-Yankee manager Joe Torre who, at the time, had just started his first managing job with the Mets. "We've all seen what Ellie does there. That's just one of a hundred different examples of why he would have been a great manager, for the Yankees or anyone else. Some people demand respect. Some command it. That was Elston Howard."

My father got it right, just as Yogi insisted. He would have adored this book. Same as he did the man about whom it was written.

—Mike Vaccaro
Sports columnist, *New York Post*

ACKNOWLEDGMENTS

THE AUTHORS WOULD LIKE TO THANK THE DOZENS OF PEOPLE WHO helped us put this book together. Over the past three years we met, visited, and talked with many of Elston's old friends and teammates, and we would like to thank them for their invaluable support.

We took trips to St. Louis, Kansas City, Los Angeles, and Cooperstown. Everywhere we turned there was someone who fondly remembered Elston. It was comforting to know that so many people still held him in such high esteem.

In St. Louis, we stayed at Arlene's old home and talked to a number of Elston's childhood friends and neighbors: Wendell Hill, Fred and Sarah Jones, Quinton Wyatt, Vito Reed, George Buchanan, Charles Irving, Martin Mathews, Ruben Buchanan, and George Dodd. Special thanks to Frank Edwards and his brother Tommy "Wheatie" Edwards for the stories they told us about their dad, Teannie Edwards. We also must thank Arlene's brother, Eddie Henley, and Arlene's sister Martha and her husband, Moses Hart, for their hospitality. Special mention must go to Vashon High School, where the gymnasium was named posthumously in honor of Elston.

A special thank-you goes to Yogi Berra and his wife, Carmen, along with Dave Kaplan, who runs Yogi's museum in Montclair, New Jersey. Whitey and Joan Ford were most delightful. We will never forget the oatmeal commercial.

We will never forget the reverence in which Elston's teammates spoke of him. At Old-Timers Day, we saw Phil Rizzuto, Al Downing, Hank Bauer, Bobby Richardson, Bill Robinson, Bill Skowron, Clete Boyer, Phil Linz, Don Larsen, Andy Carey, Bobby Murcer, Joe Pepitone, Charlie Silvera, Bobby Shantz, Jerry Coleman, and Ralph Houk.

We'd like to thank George Steinbrenner, Ron Guidry, Goose Gossage, Mike Wallace, Fritz Peterson, Frank Messer, and Gene Michael. We also would like to thank Jim Kaat, Bill White, Herb Score, Larry Doby, Bill Virdon, Reggie Smith, Bill Rohr, and Don Newcombe.

When we went to Kansas City, we visited the Negro Hall of Fame. We were blessed and amazed by Buck O'Neil's enthusiasm and warmness as he drove us to our hotel after a memorable dinner at his favorite rib joint. Special thanks also go to Phil Dixon, Connie Johnson, and Sam Adams for their help.

Many of our photographs were given to us by the late Bob Olen, the former Yankee and *New York Post* photographer.

Special thanks go out to Los Angeles TV personality Tom Reed, Elston's cousin, and to "Members Only Television" for providing us with the basis of Don Newcombe's memorable foreword.

We also must thank Barbara Wood for cataloging Elston's personal papers and library, the late Fran Miller who, before she died in the summer of 2000, gave us so many memories involving the Howard family and the personal notes and papers of her beloved husband, Bernie, the publisher of *Gentleman's Quarterly*.

In Cooperstown, we must thank Marj and Ed Landers at the White House Inn for giving us shelter on cold nights. The late Dale LaFond deserves mention for his hospitality and friendship. And we cannot forget Jeff Idelson, Tim Wiles, and the rest of the gang for their help at the Baseball Hall of Fame.

Thanks also must go to Frank Hamilton, Leonard Stone, Sheldon Stone, the Rev. Jesse Jackson, George Crowe, Sasha Nichelson, Alan Kushner, Tom Keegan, Phil Mushnick, Bill Kane, Carl Schurtz, Phyllis Merighe, Ed Stackler, Grace Renna, Chris Gargano, Bob McCord, and David Viglione.

Lastly, this book would not have been possible without the help of Cheryl Howard and C. Bette Wimbish. We love you!

BIBLIOGRAPHY

Allen, Maury. *You Could Look It Up: The Life of Casey Stengel.*
Creamer, Robert. *Casey Stengel.*
Dixon, Phil, and Patrick Hannigan. *Negro League Baseball, a Photographic History.*
Ford, Whitey. *Slick.*
Halberstam, David. *October 1964.*
Houk, Ralph, and Robert Creamer. *Season of Glory.*
Moffi, Larry, and Jonathan Kronstadt. *Crossing the Line: Black Major Leaguers, 1947–1959.*
O'Neil, Buck. *I Was Right on Time.*
Rust, Art Jr. *Get That Nigger Off the Field.*
Tygiel, Jules. *Baseball's Great Experiment.*

Reference material included news clippings from the *New York Post* library, the Baseball Hall of Fame library, and the *Sporting News*.

Index